Alone Forever

The Singles Collection

BY LIZ PRINCE

Alone Forever, the Singles Collection
© 2014 LIZ PRINCE

TOP SHELF PRODUCTIONS
P.O. Box 1282
Marietta, GA 30061-1282
U.S.A.

Publishers: Brett Warnock and Chris Staros
Top Shelf Productions® and the Top Shelf logo
are registered trademarks of Top Shelf
Productions, INC.

Visit our online catalog @
www.topshelfcomix.com

First Printing, February 2014

Printed in Canada

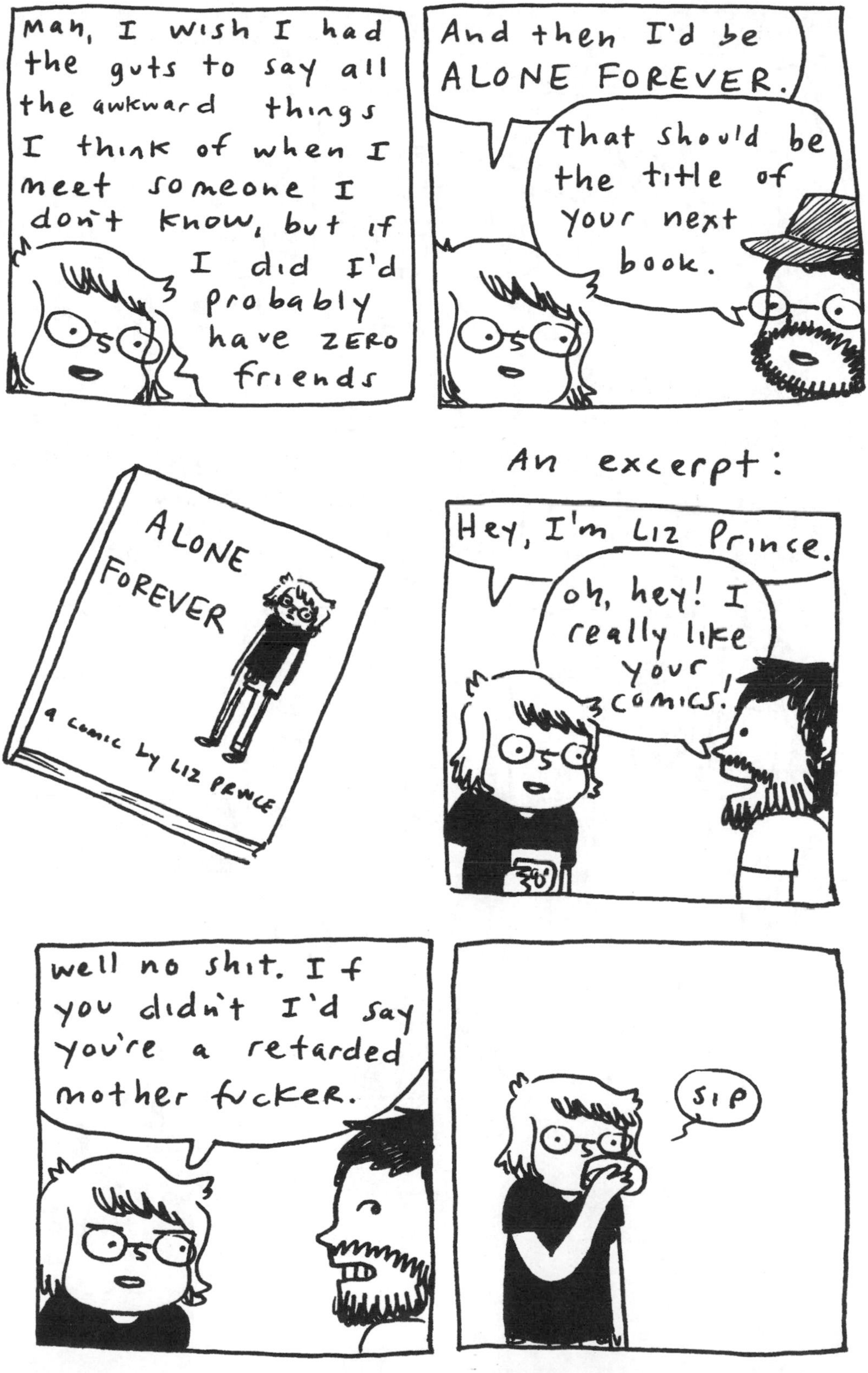
Man, I wish I had the guts to say all the awkward things I think of when I meet someone I don't know, but if I did I'd probably have ZERO friends
And then I'd be ALONE FOREVER.
That should be the title of your next book.
ALONE FOREVER
A COMIC BY LIZ PRINCE
An excerpt:
Hey, I'm Liz Prince.
oh, hey! I really like your comics!
well no shit. If you didn't I'd say you're a retarded mother fucker.
SIP

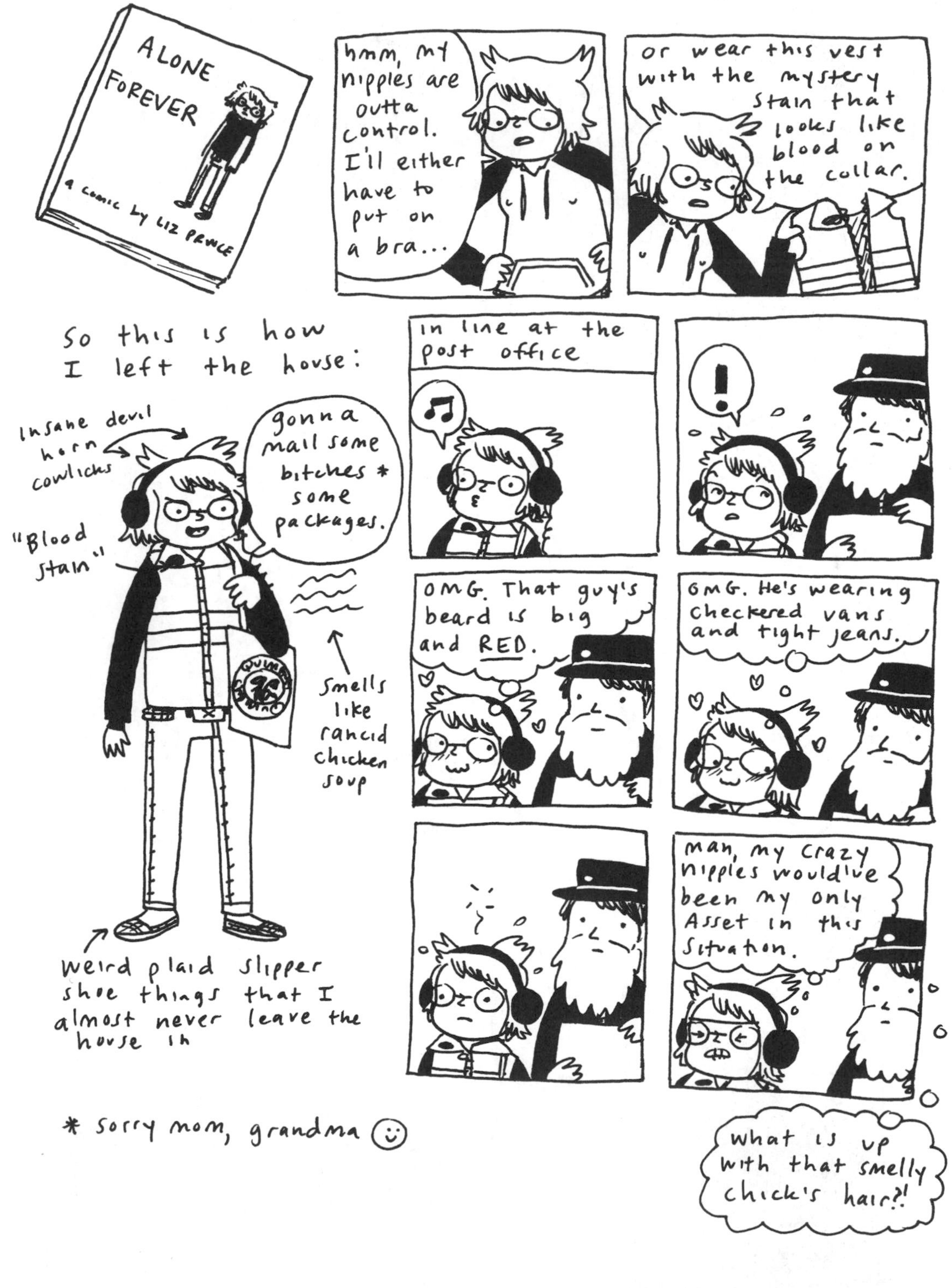
ALONE FOREVER
a comic by LIZ PRINCE
hmm, my nipples are outta control. I'll either have to put on a bra...
or wear this vest with the mystery stain that looks like blood on the collar.
So this is how I left the house:
insane devil horn cowlicks
gonna mail some bitches * some packages.
"Blood stain"
smells like rancid chicken soup
weird plaid slipper shoe things that I almost never leave the house in
* sorry mom, grandma
in line at the post office
!
OMG. That guy's beard is big and RED.
OMG. He's wearing checkered vans and tight jeans.
man, my crazy nipples would've been my only asset in this situation.
what is up with that smelly chick's hair?!

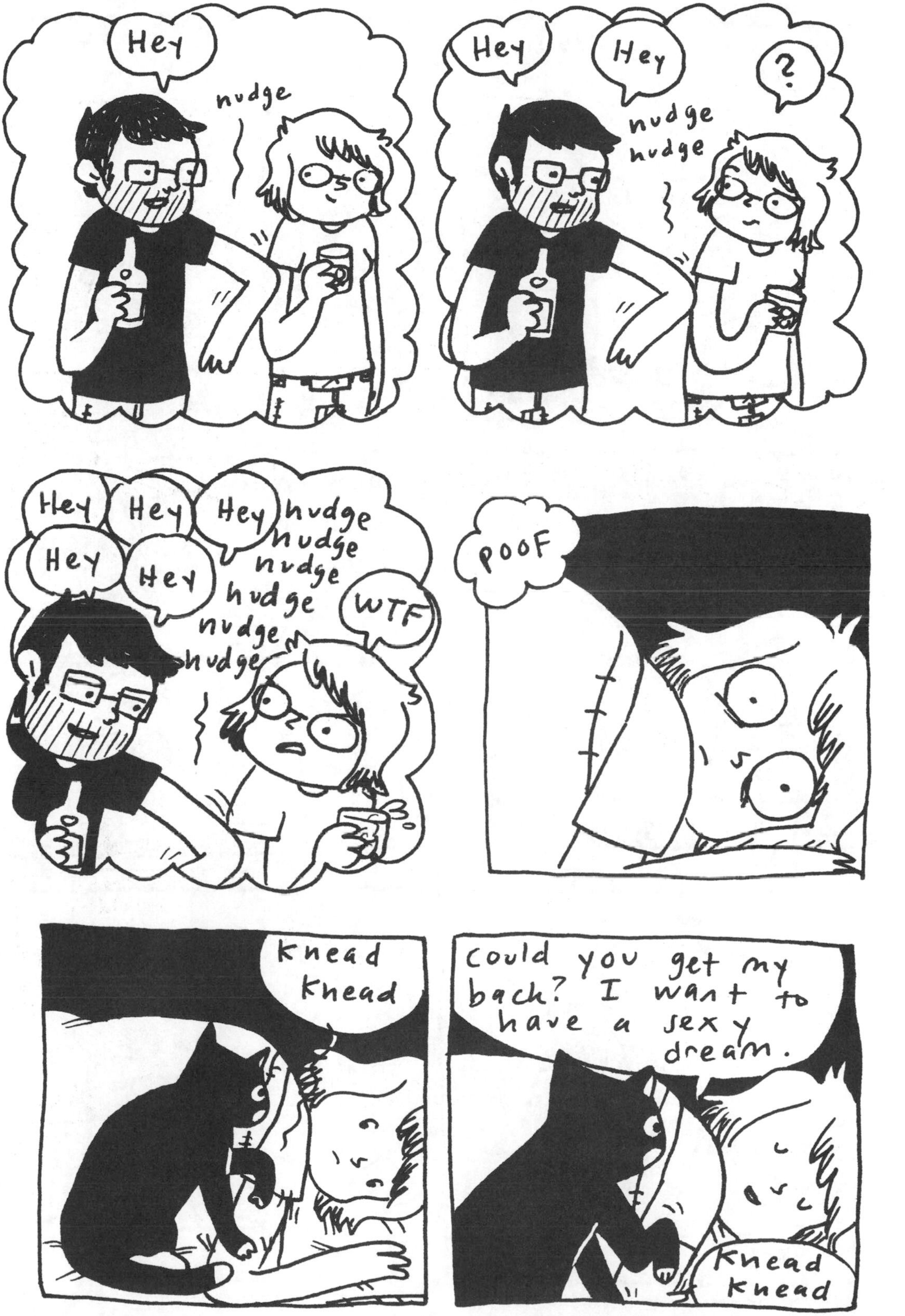

Hey
nudge
Hey
Hey
?
nudge
nudge
Hey
Hey
Hey
Hey
Hey
nudge
nudge
nudge
nudge
nudge
nudge
WTF
POOF
Knead
Knead
Could you get my back? I want to have a sexy dream.
Knead
Knead

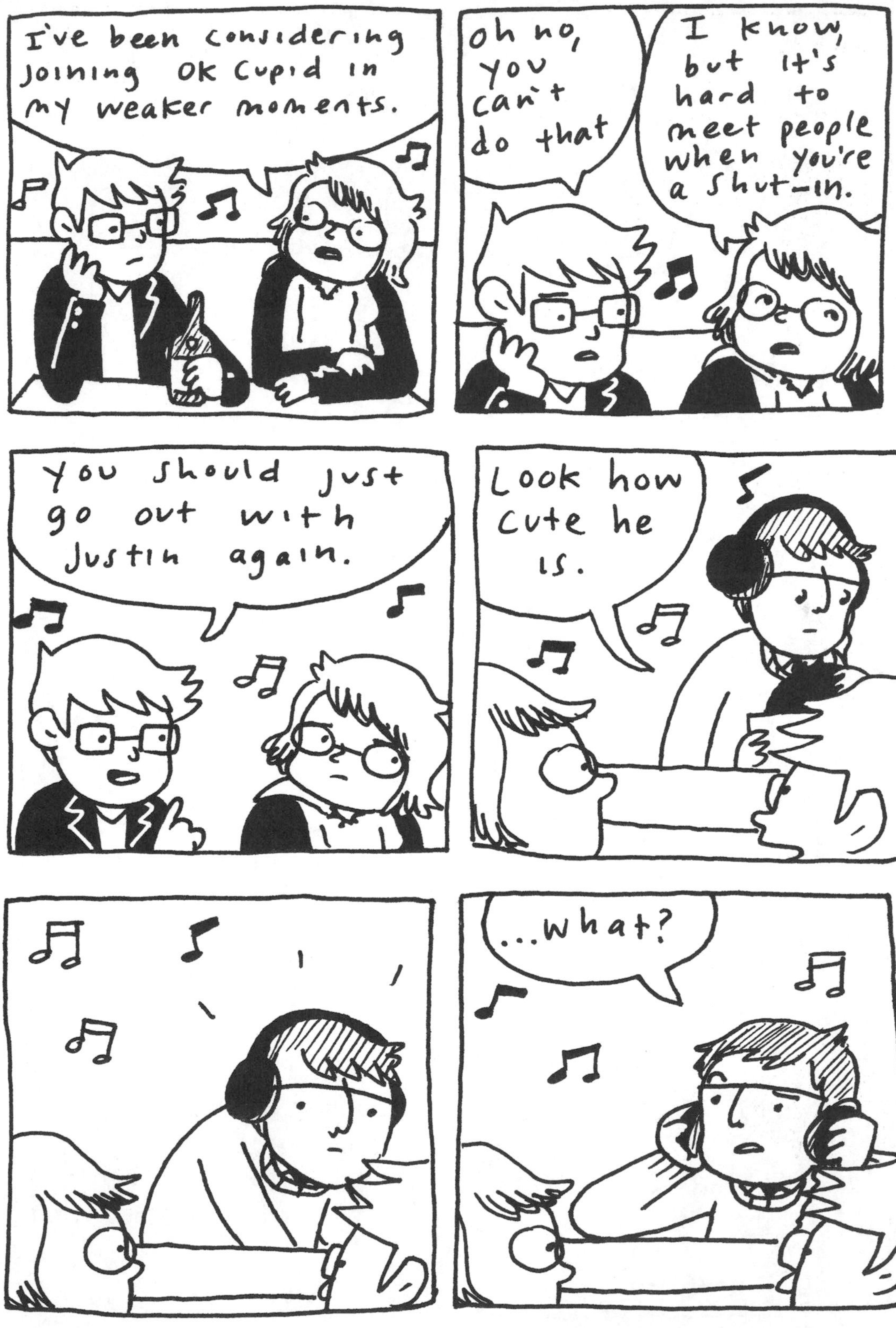
I've been considering joining OK Cupid in my weaker moments.
oh no, you can't do that
I know, but it's hard to meet people when you're a shut-in.
you should just go out with Justin again.
Look how cute he is.
...what?

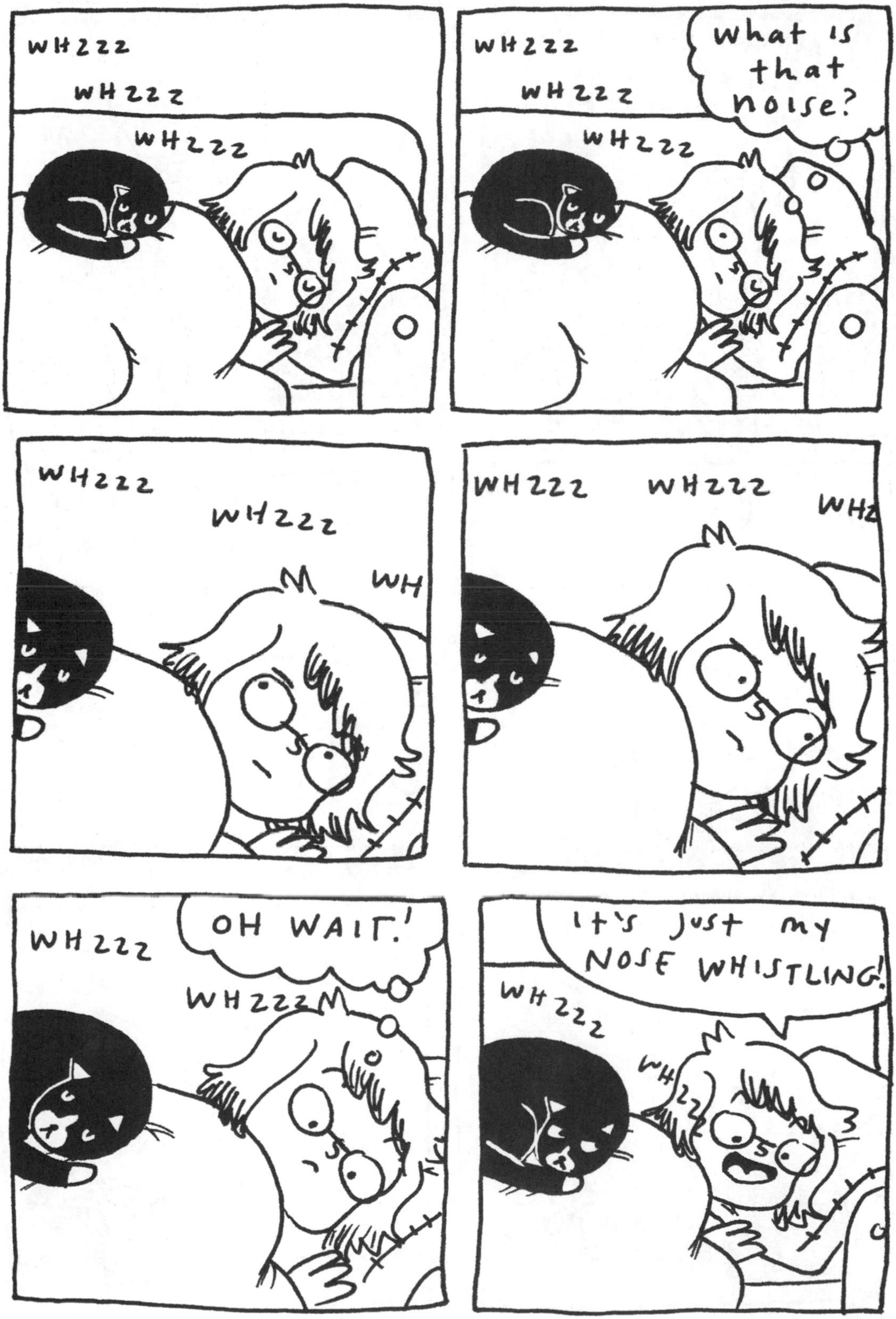
WHZZZ
WHZZZ
WHZZZ
WHZZZ
WHZZZ
WHZZZ
What is that noise?
WHZZZ
WHZZZ
WH
WHZZZ
WHZZZ
WHZ
WHZZZ
OH WAIT!
WHZZZM
It's just my NOSE WHISTLING!
WHZZZ
WHZZZ

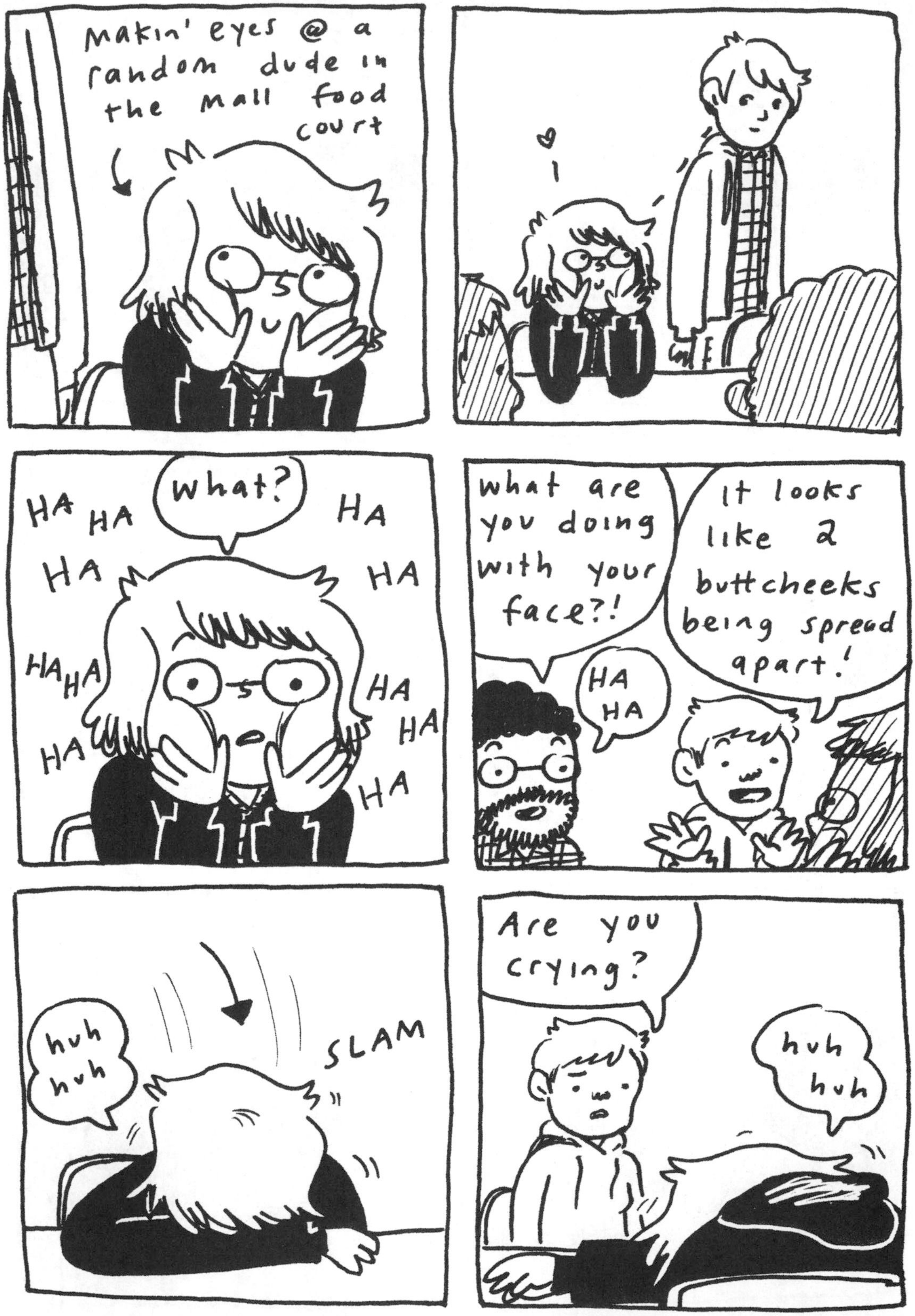
Makin' eyes @ a random dude in the mall food court
what?
HA HA HA HA HA HA HA HA HA HA HA HA HA
what are you doing with your face?!
HA HA
It looks like 2 buttcheeks being spread apart!
huh huh
SLAM
Are you crying?
huh huh

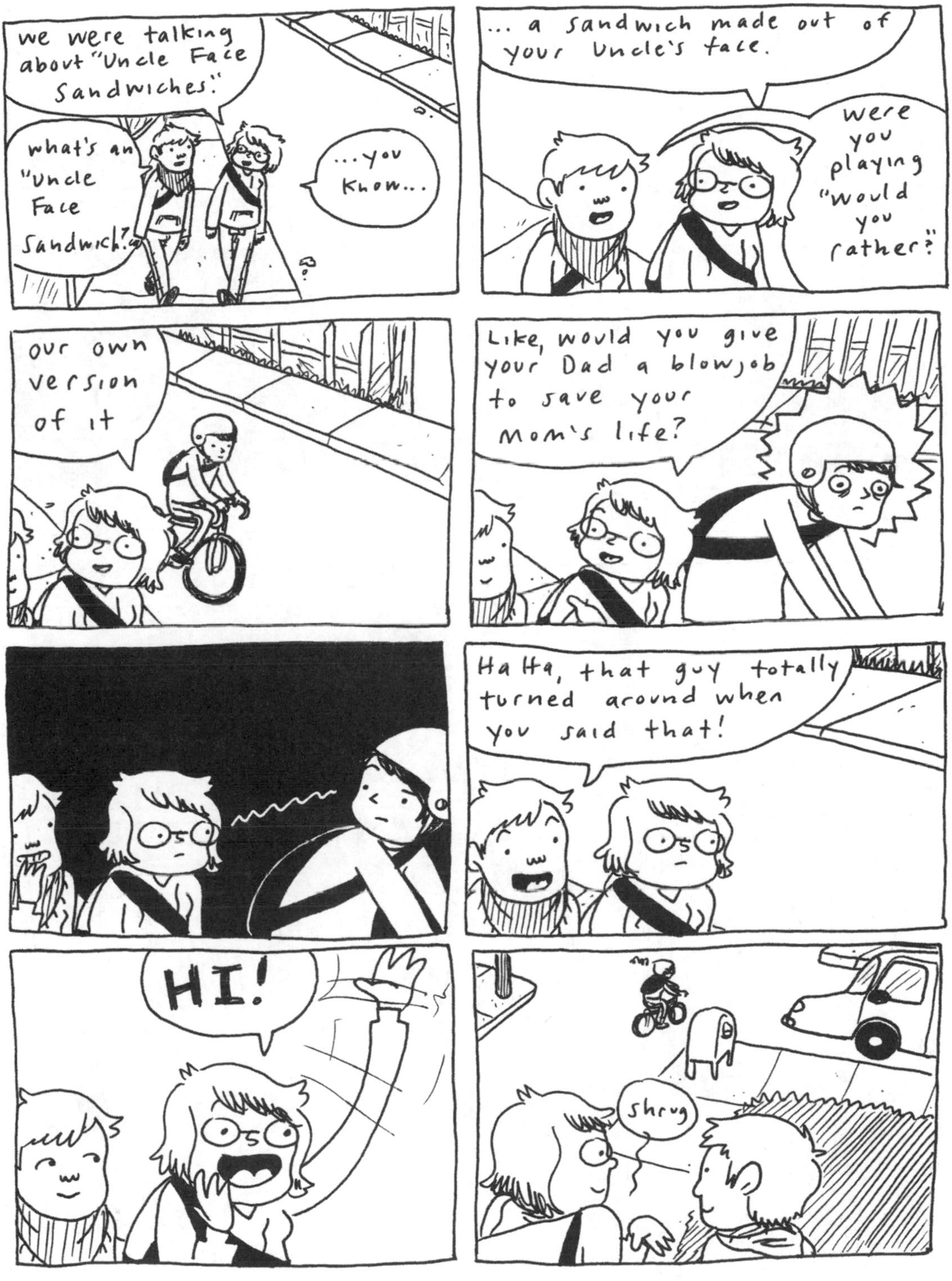
we were talking about "Uncle Face Sandwiches."
what's an "Uncle Face Sandwich?"
...you know...
... a sandwich made out of your Uncle's face.
were you playing "would you rather?"
our own version of it
Like, would you give your Dad a blowjob to save your Mom's life?
HaHa, that guy totally turned around when you said that!
HI!
shrug

I HAVE BEEN EATING A LOT OF GARLIC

It makes my clothes smell like garlic

ew

SNIFF

a hoodie I was planning on never washing

It makes my breath smell like garlic

sorry dinner was so garlicky last night

I woke up this morning and it was like someone took a garlic shit in my mouth.

It even makes my arm-pits smell like garlic

ok, WTF?

But at least I don't have to worry about this

DING DONG

My word, a caller? at this hour?

CHICK LIT

LIZ! I left Bella, you have to run away with me!

SLAM

NEVER! you pretty-boy-lisa-frank excuse for a vampire!

But I do have to worry about this

nom nom

COUNT CHOCULA

what's that awful smell?

?

I'm outta here!

COUNT CHOCULA

WAKKA WAKKA

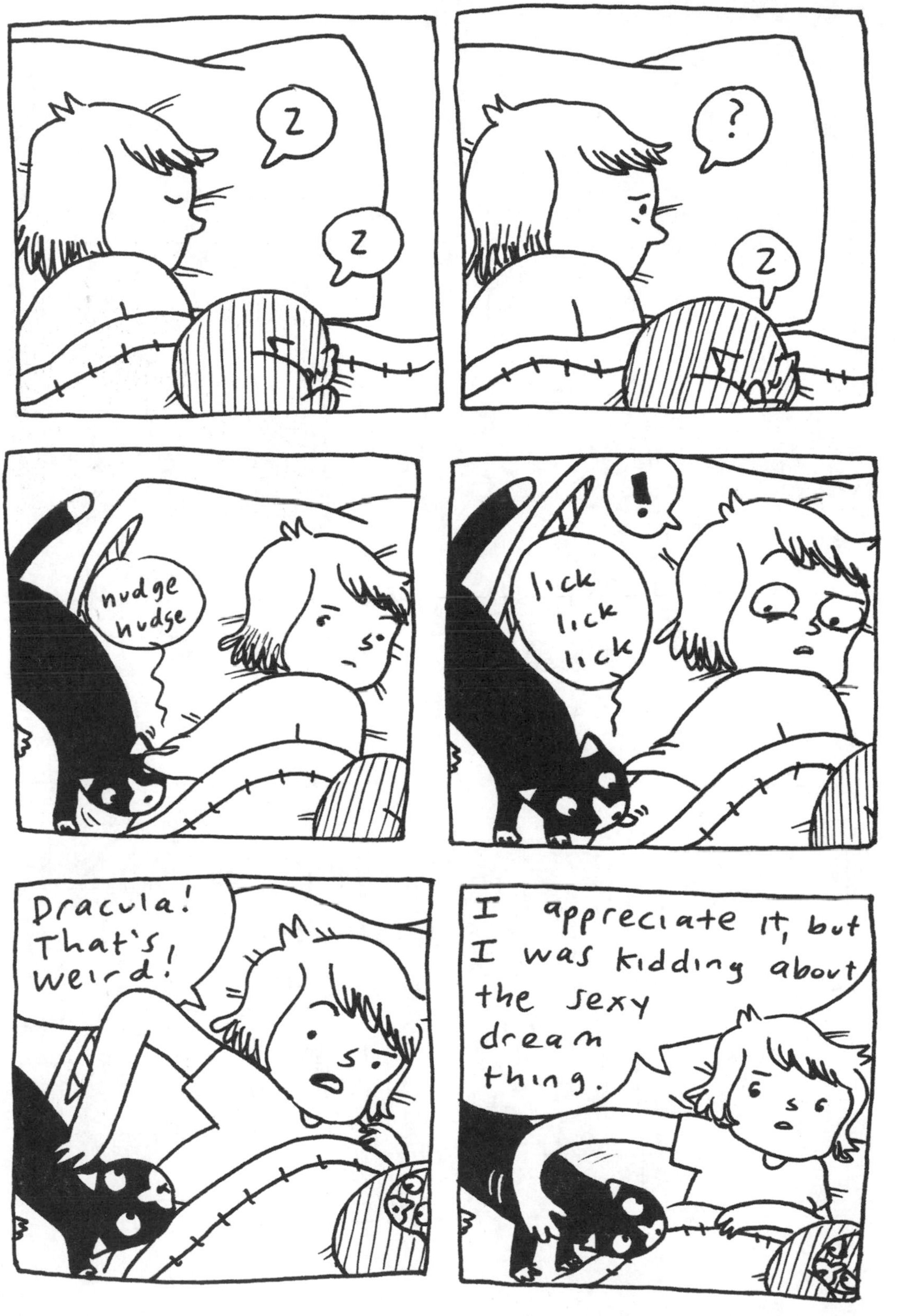

Z
Z
?
Z
nudge nudge
!
lick lick lick
Dracula! That's weird!
I appreciate it, but I was kidding about the sexy dream thing.

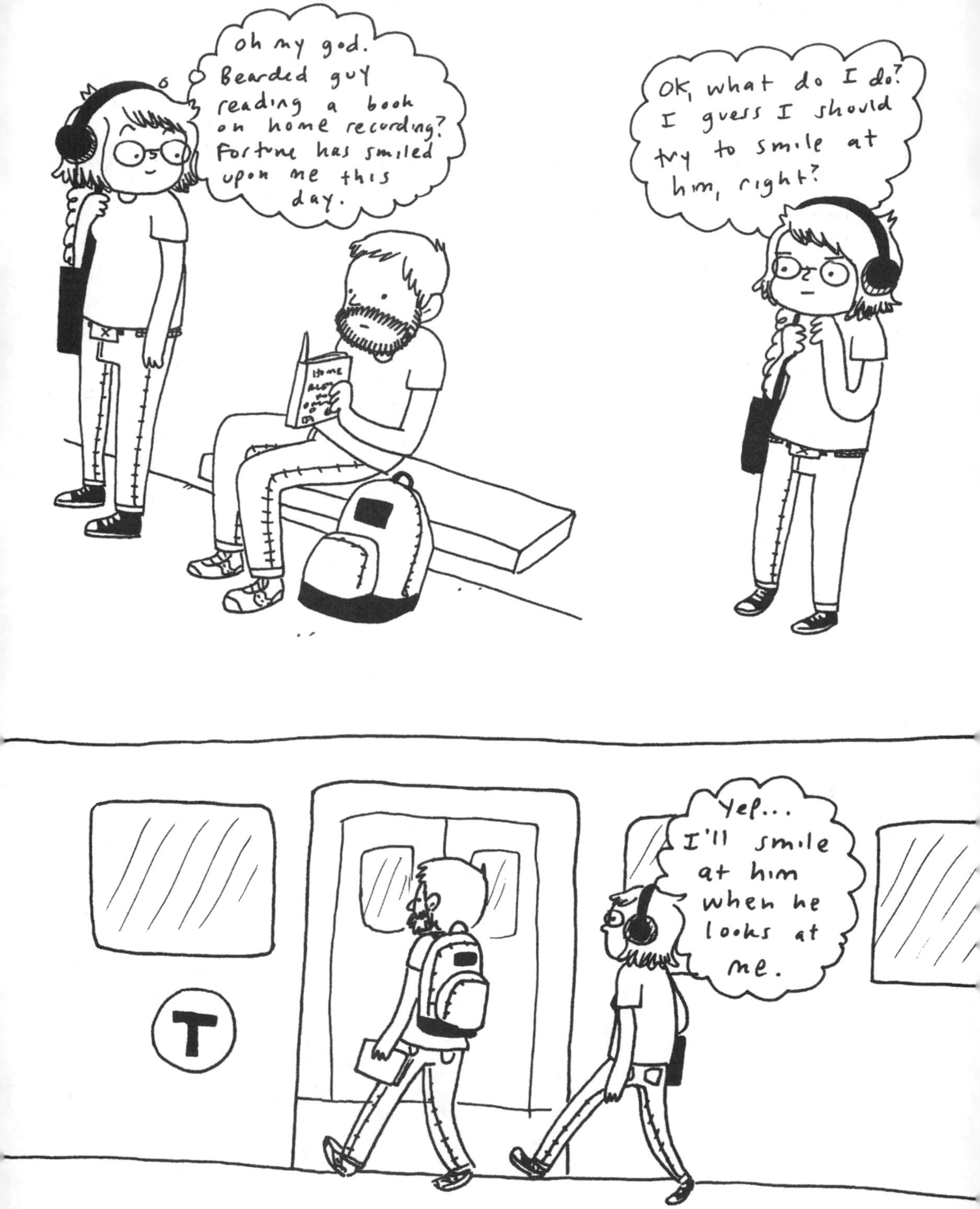
oh my god. Bearded guy reading a book on home recording? Fortune has smiled upon me this day.
Ok, what do I do? I guess I should try to smile at him, right?
Yep... I'll smile at him when he looks at me.

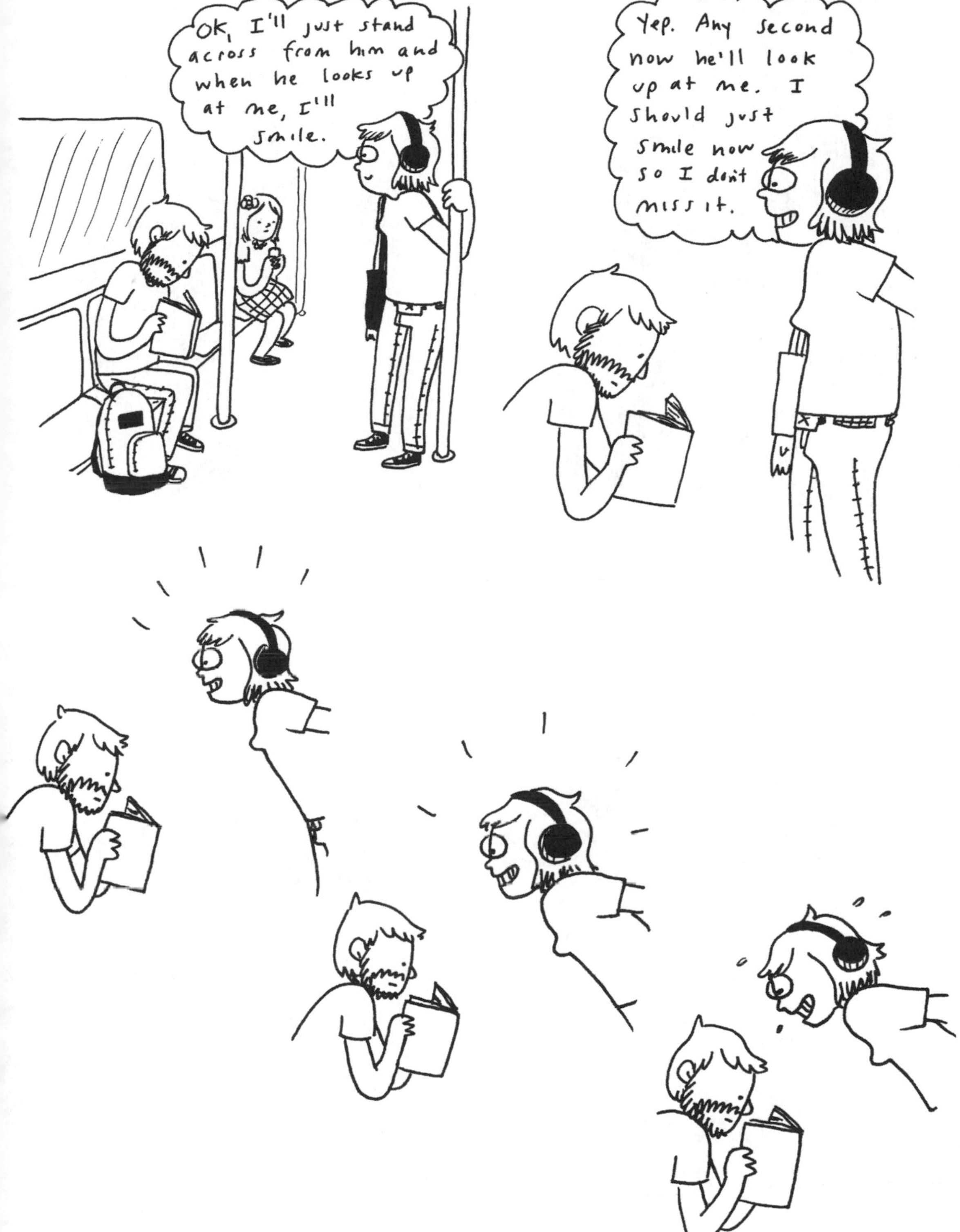
Ok, I'll just stand across from him and when he looks up at me, I'll smile.
Yep. Any second now he'll look up at me. I should just smile now so I don't miss it.

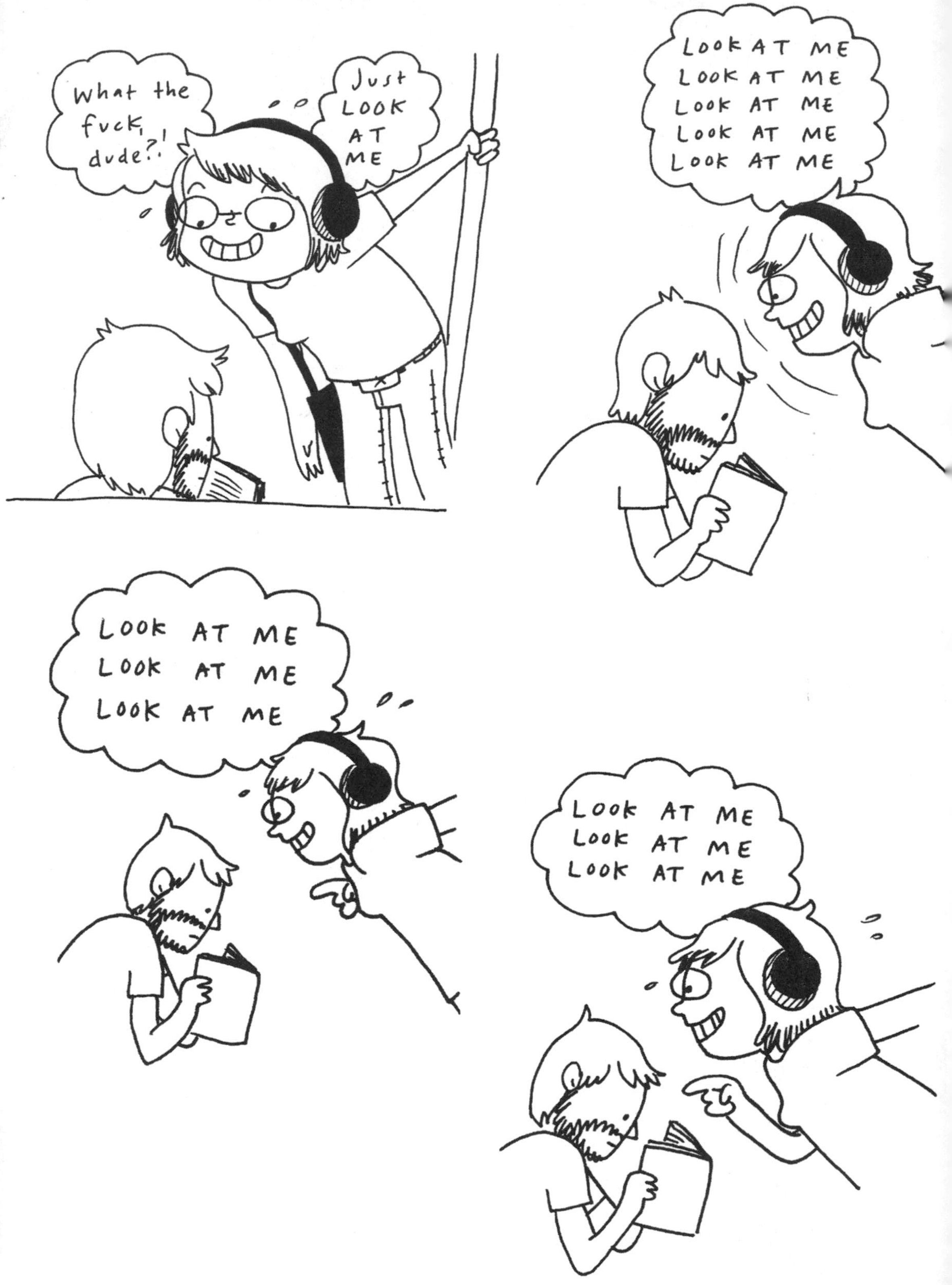
What the fuck, dude?!
Just LOOK AT ME
LOOK AT ME LOOK AT ME LOOK AT ME LOOK AT ME LOOK AT ME
LOOK AT ME LOOK AT ME LOOK AT ME
LOOK AT ME LOOK AT ME LOOK AT ME

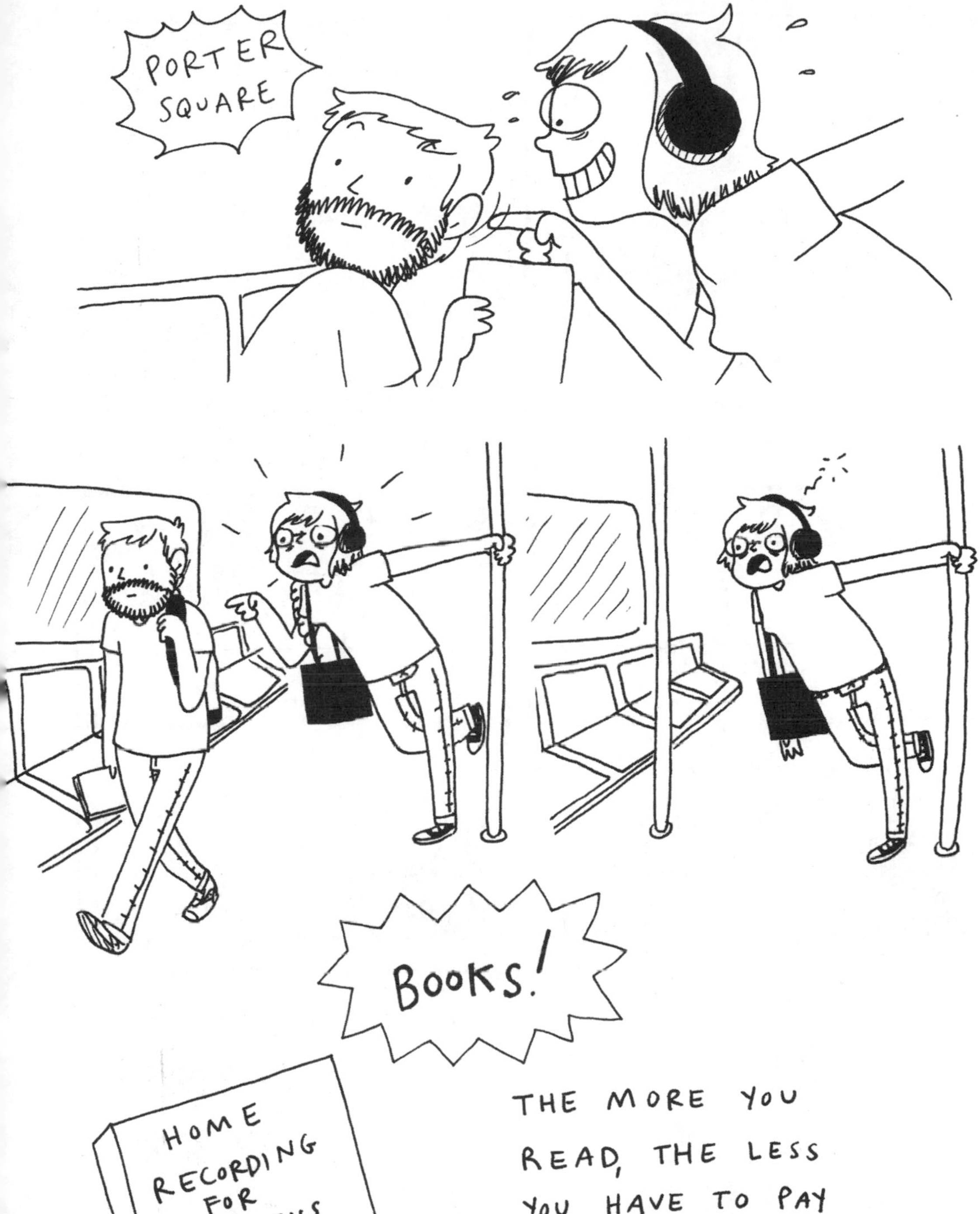
PORTER SQUARE
BOOKS!
HOME RECORDING FOR OBLIVIOUS DUDES
THE MORE YOU READ, THE LESS YOU HAVE TO PAY ATTENTION TO CREEPY PEOPLE ON THE SUBWAY.

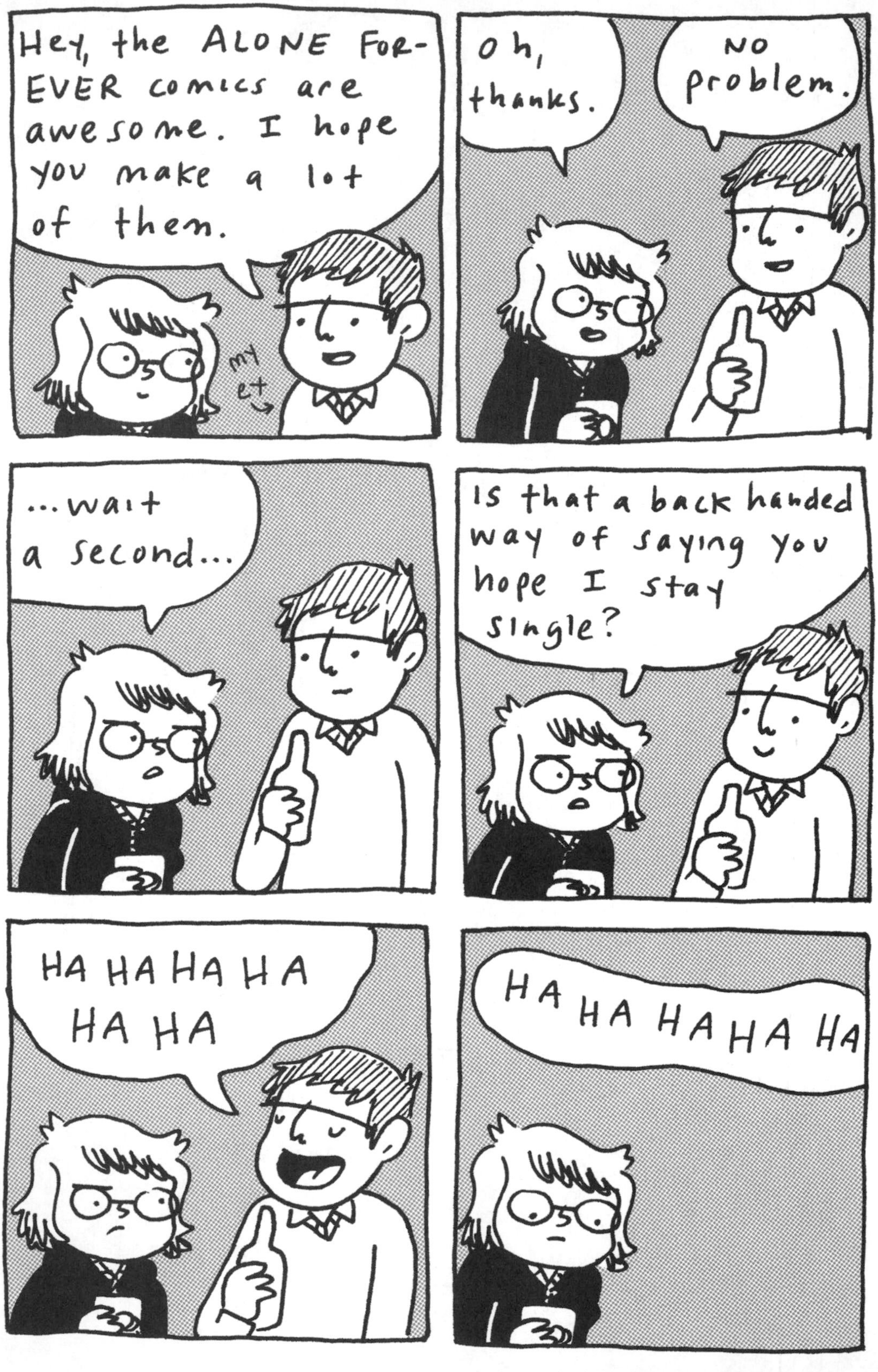
Hey, the ALONE FOREVER comics are awesome. I hope you make a lot of them.
my ex
Oh, thanks.
NO problem.
...wait a second...
Is that a back handed way of saying you hope I stay single?
HA HA HA HA HA HA HA
HA HA HA HA HA HA

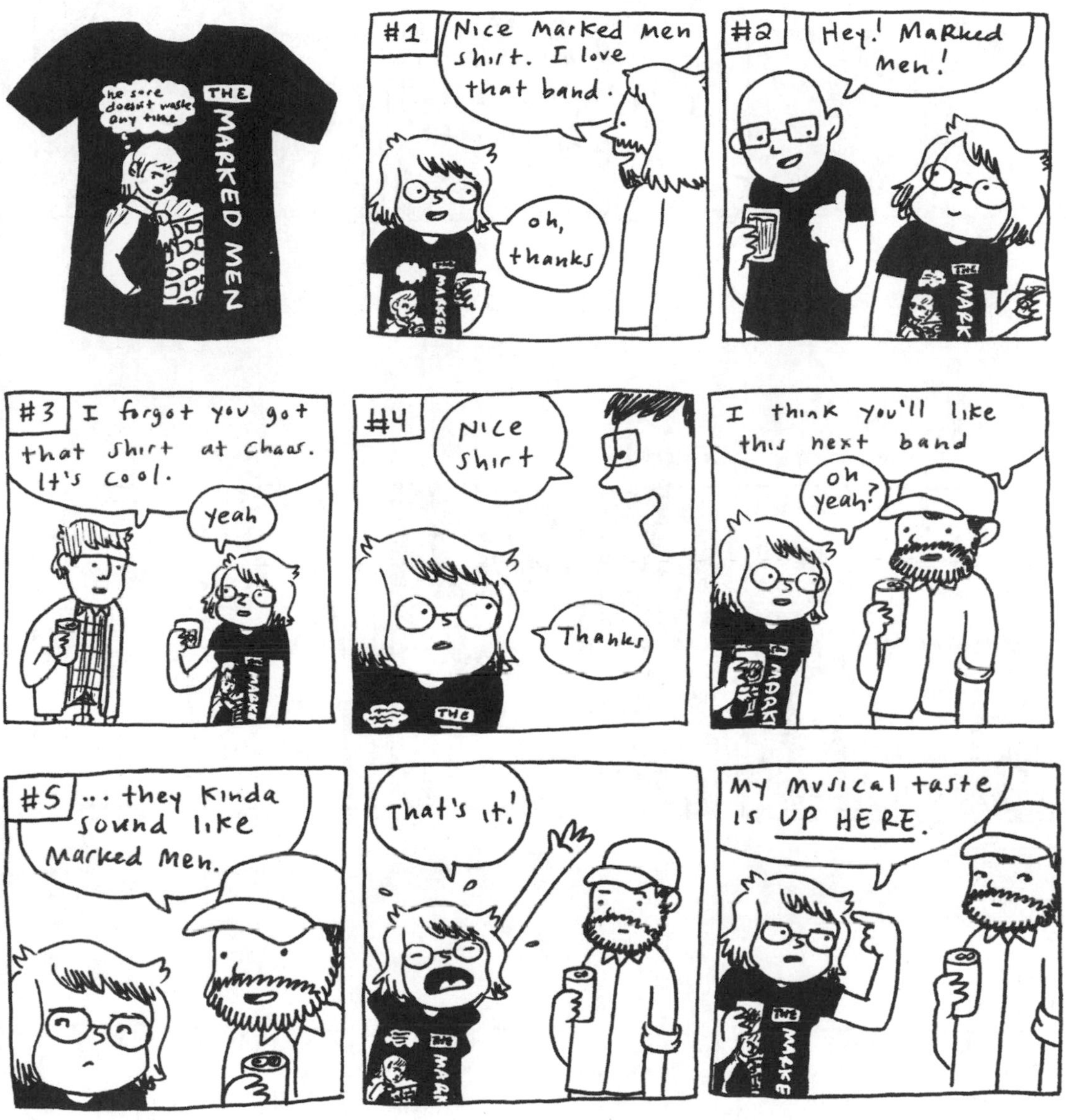
he sure doesn't waste any time
THE MARKED MEN
#1
Nice Marked Men shirt. I love that band.
oh, thanks
#2
Hey! Marked Men!
#3
I forgot you got that shirt at Chaos. It's cool.
yeah
#4
Nice shirt
Thanks
I think you'll like this next band
oh yeah?
#5
... they kinda sound like Marked Men.
That's it!
My musical taste is UP HERE.

just kidding: I know nobody was looking at my tits because they are rather unimpressive.

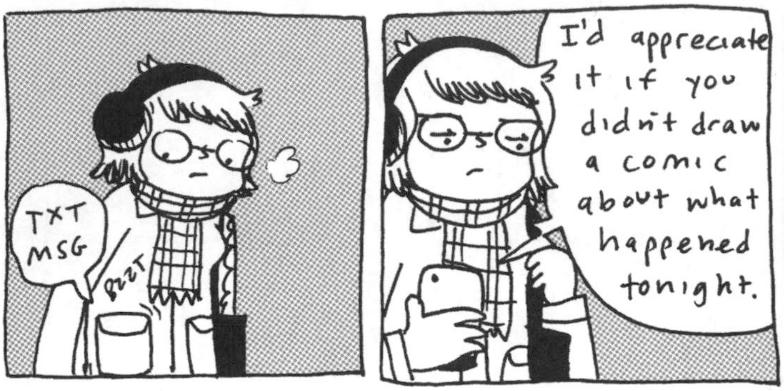
TXT MSG
BZZT
I'd appreciate it if you didn't draw a comic about what happened tonight.
WELL
DUH

Total doppelbanger material

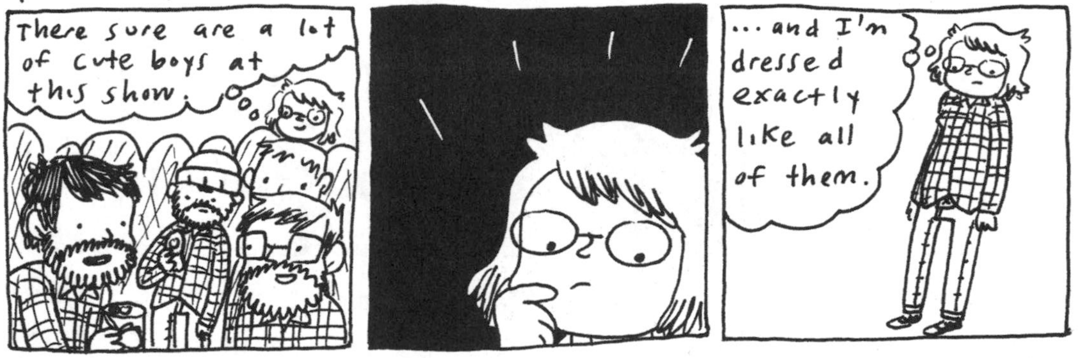
There sure are a lot of cute boys at this show.
...and I'm dressed exactly like all of them.

Alone for a few hours

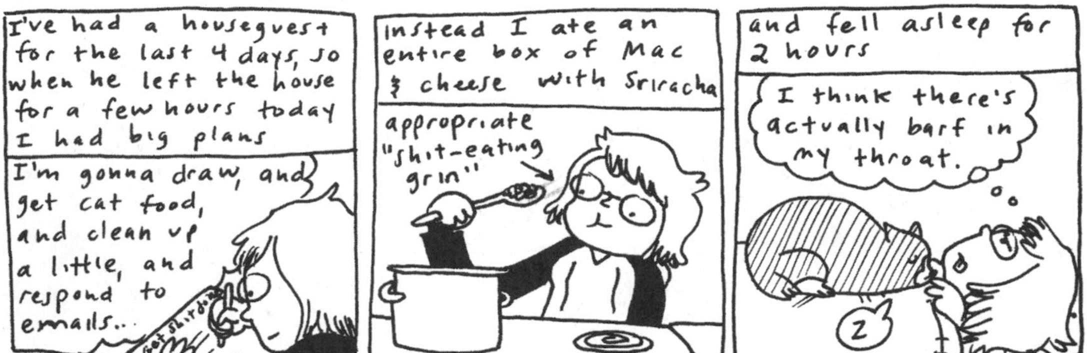
I've had a houseguest for the last 4 days, so when he left the house for a few hours today I had big plans
I'm gonna draw, and get cat food, and clean up a little, and respond to emails...
Making a "to-do" list
instead I ate an entire box of Mac & cheese with Sriracha
appropriate "shit-eating grin"
and fell asleep for 2 hours
I think there's actually barf in my throat.
Z

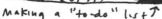

MEET THE GIRL WHO IS HIDING IN YOUR BUSHES

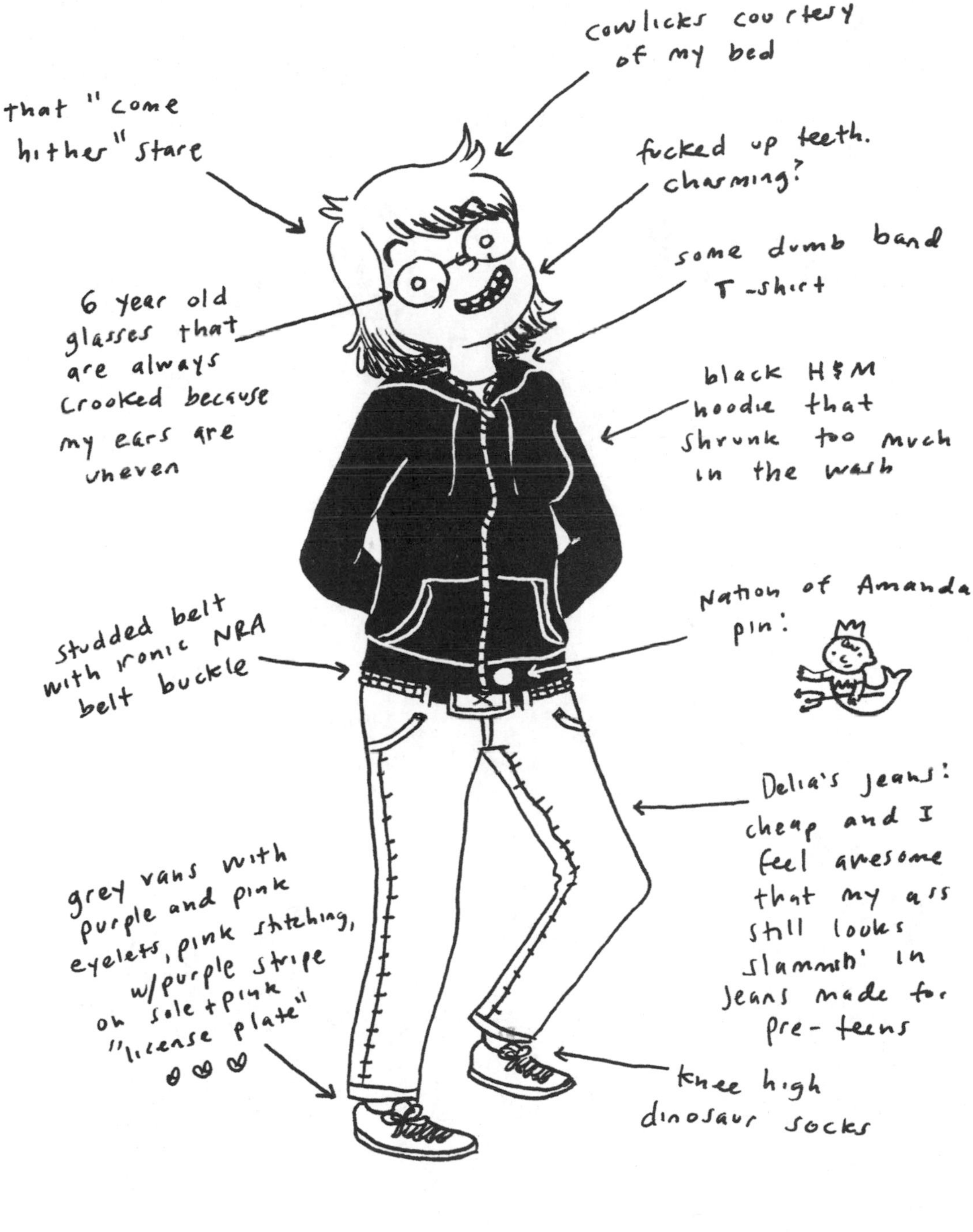

cowlicks courtesy of my bed
that "come hither" stare
fucked up teeth. charming?
some dumb band T-shirt
6 year old glasses that are always crooked because my ears are uneven
black H&M hoodie that shrunk too much in the wash
Nation of Amanda pin:
studded belt with ironic NRA belt buckle
Delia's jeans: cheap and I feel awesome that my ass still looks slammin' in jeans made for pre-teens
grey vans with purple and pink eyelets, pink stitching, w/purple stripe on sole + pink "license plate"
knee high dinosaur socks

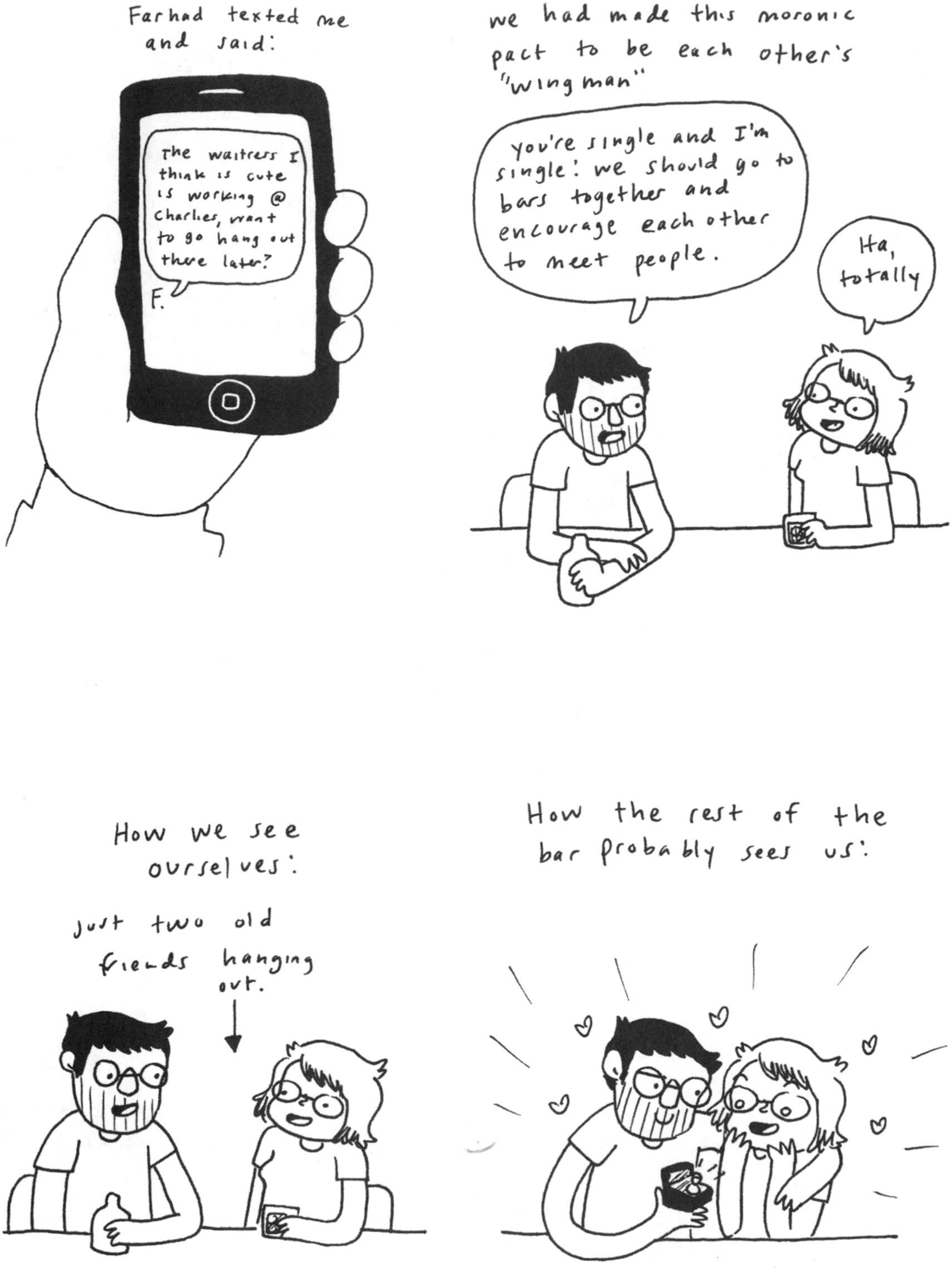
Farhad texted me and said:
The waitress I think is cute is working @ Charlie's, want to go hang out there later?
F.
we had made this moronic pact to be each other's "wingman"
you're single and I'm single: we should go to bars together and encourage each other to meet people.
Ha, totally
How we see ourselves:
just two old friends hanging out.
How the rest of the bar probably sees us:

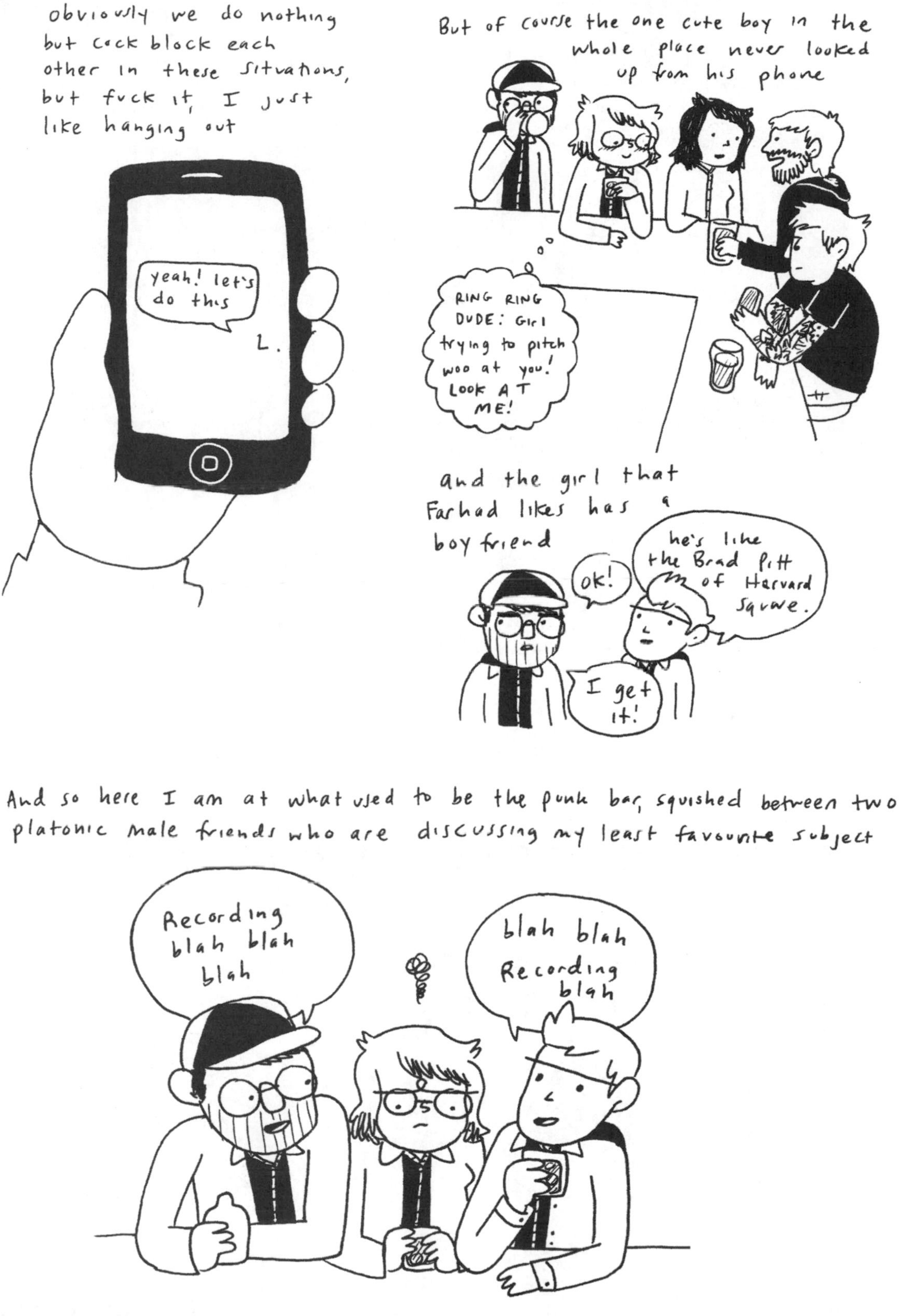
obviously we do nothing but cock block each other in these situations, but fuck it, I just like hanging out
yeah! let's do this
L.
But of course the one cute boy in the whole place never looked up from his phone
RING RING DUDE: Girl trying to pitch woo at you! LOOK AT ME!
and the girl that Farhad likes has a boyfriend
OK!
he's like the Brad Pitt of Harvard Square.
I get it!
And so here I am at what used to be the punk bar, squished between two platonic male friends who are discussing my least favourite subject
Recording blah blah blah
blah blah Recording blah

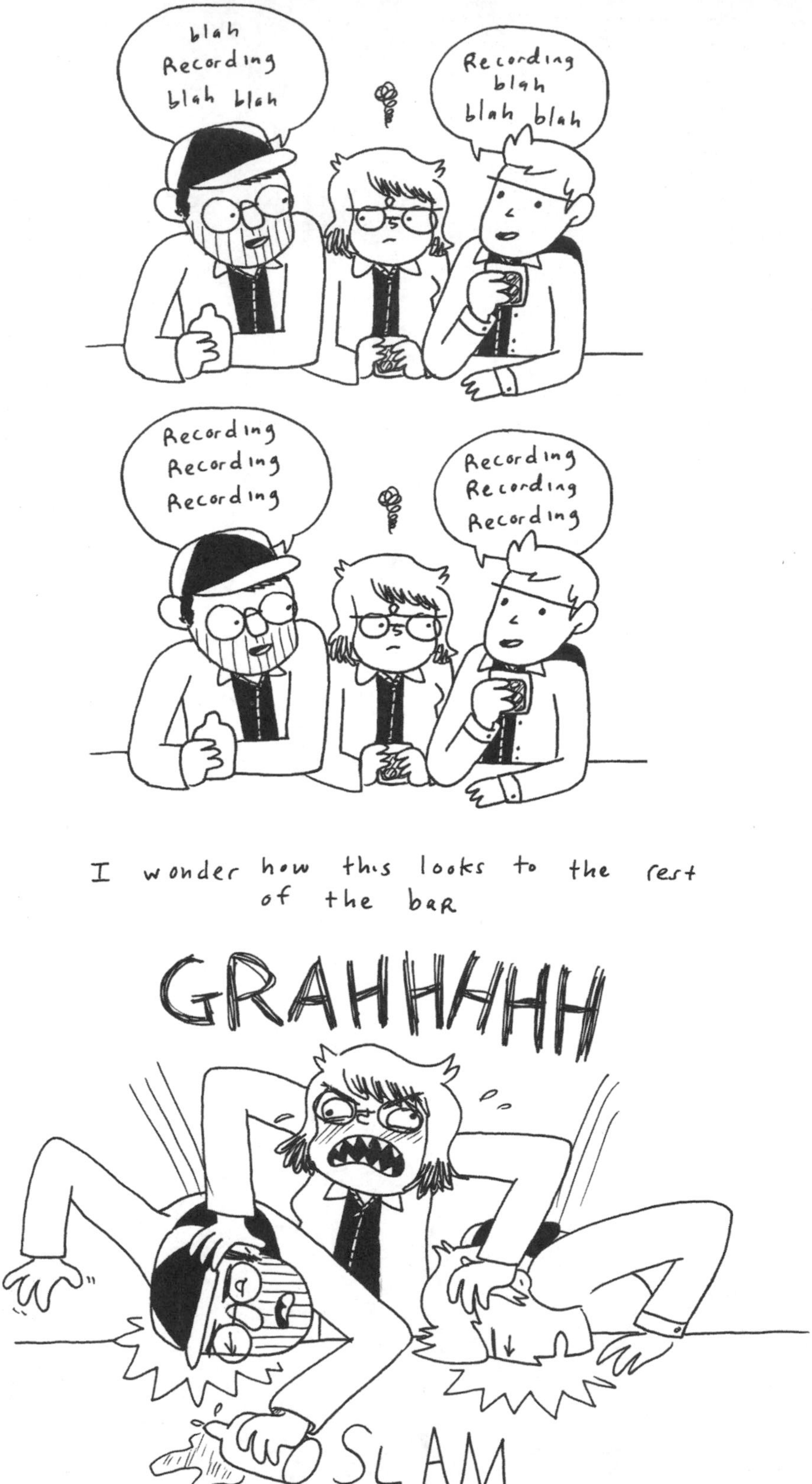
blah Recording blah blah
Recording blah blah blah
Recording Recording Recording
Recording Recording Recording
I wonder how this looks to the rest of the bar
GRAHHHHH
SLAM

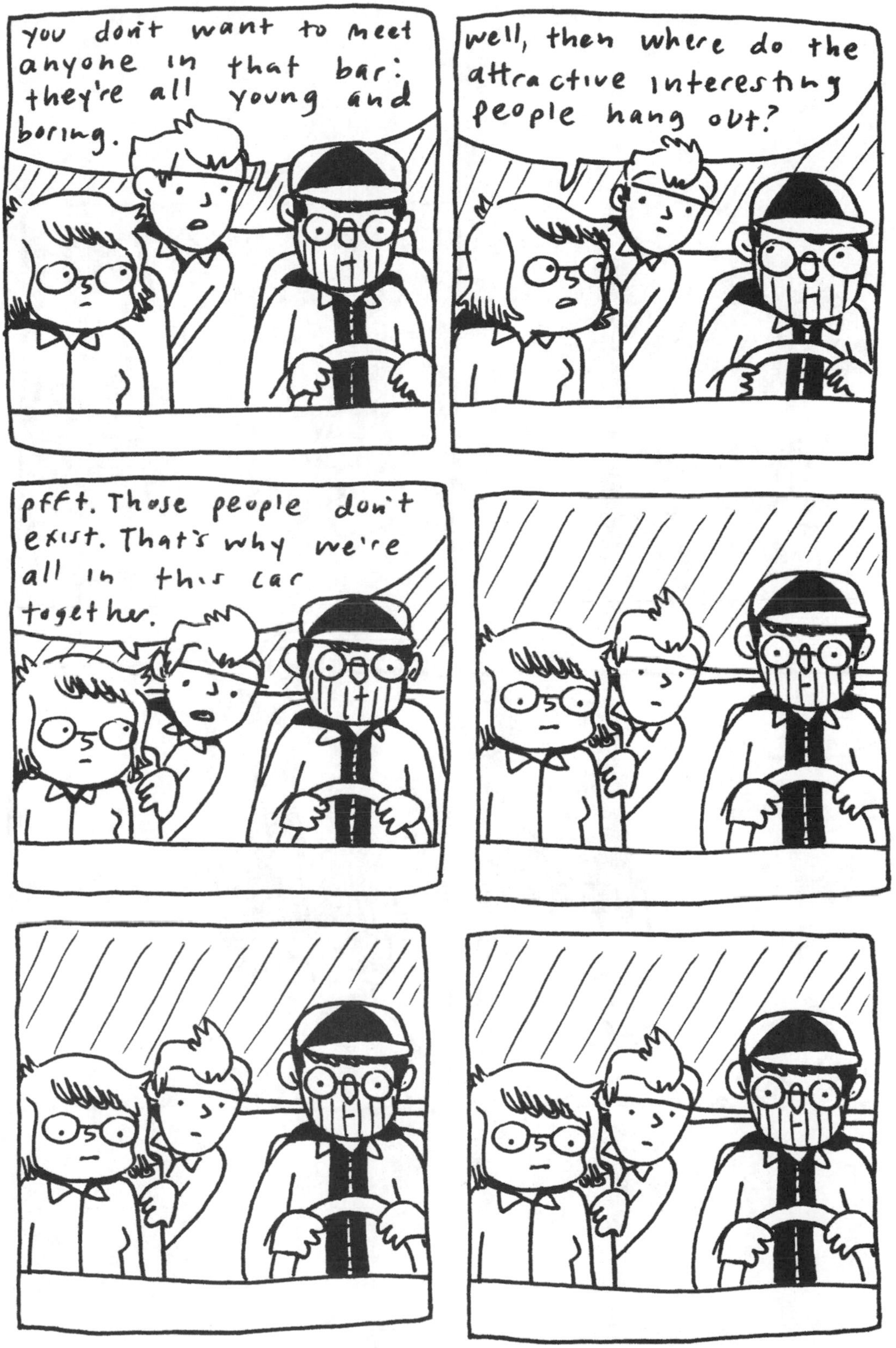
you don't want to meet anyone in that bar: they're all young and boring.
well, then where do the attractive interesting people hang out?
pfft. Those people don't exist. That's why we're all in this car together.

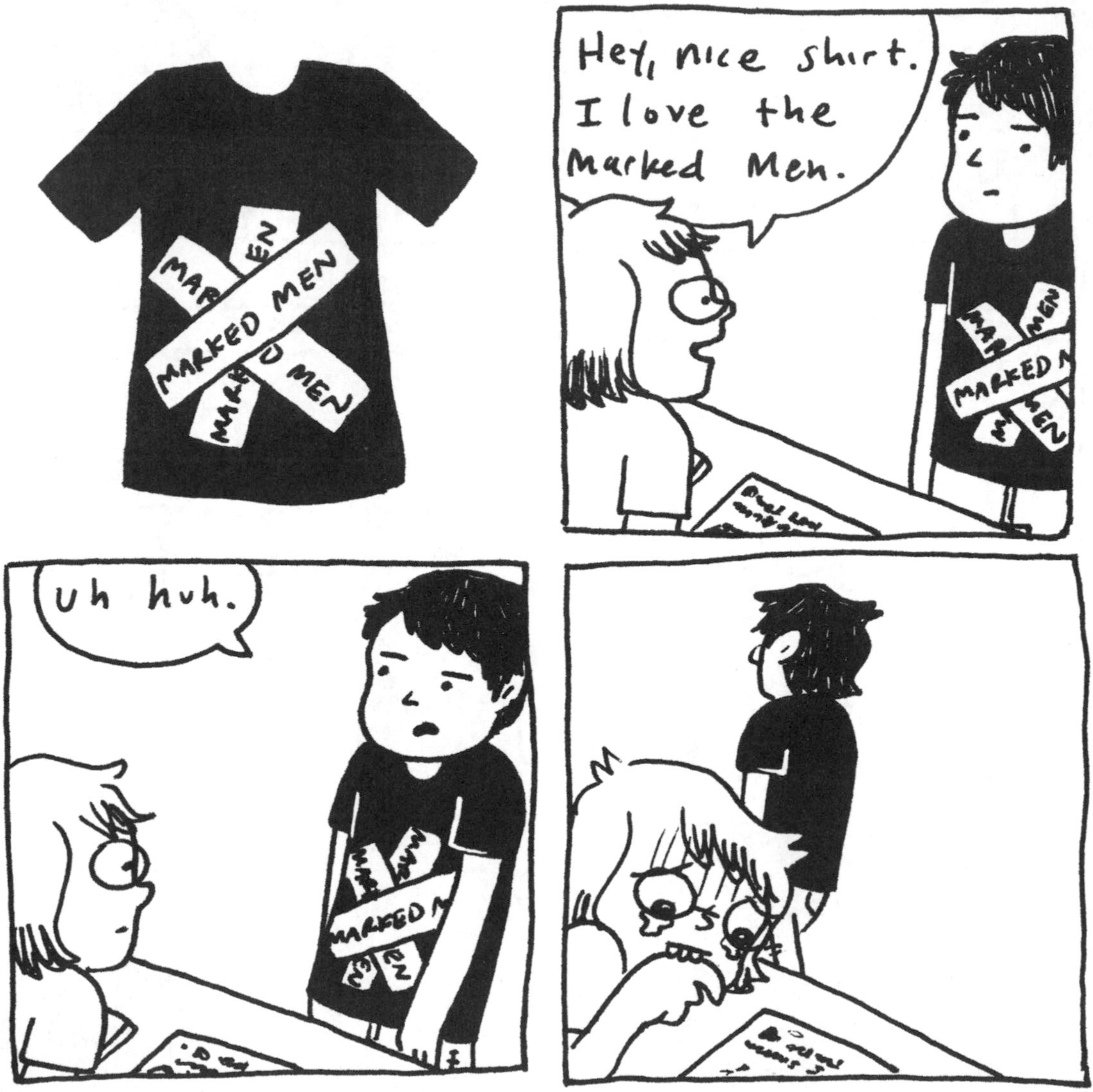
MARKED MEN
Hey, nice shirt. I love the Marked Men.
Uh huh.

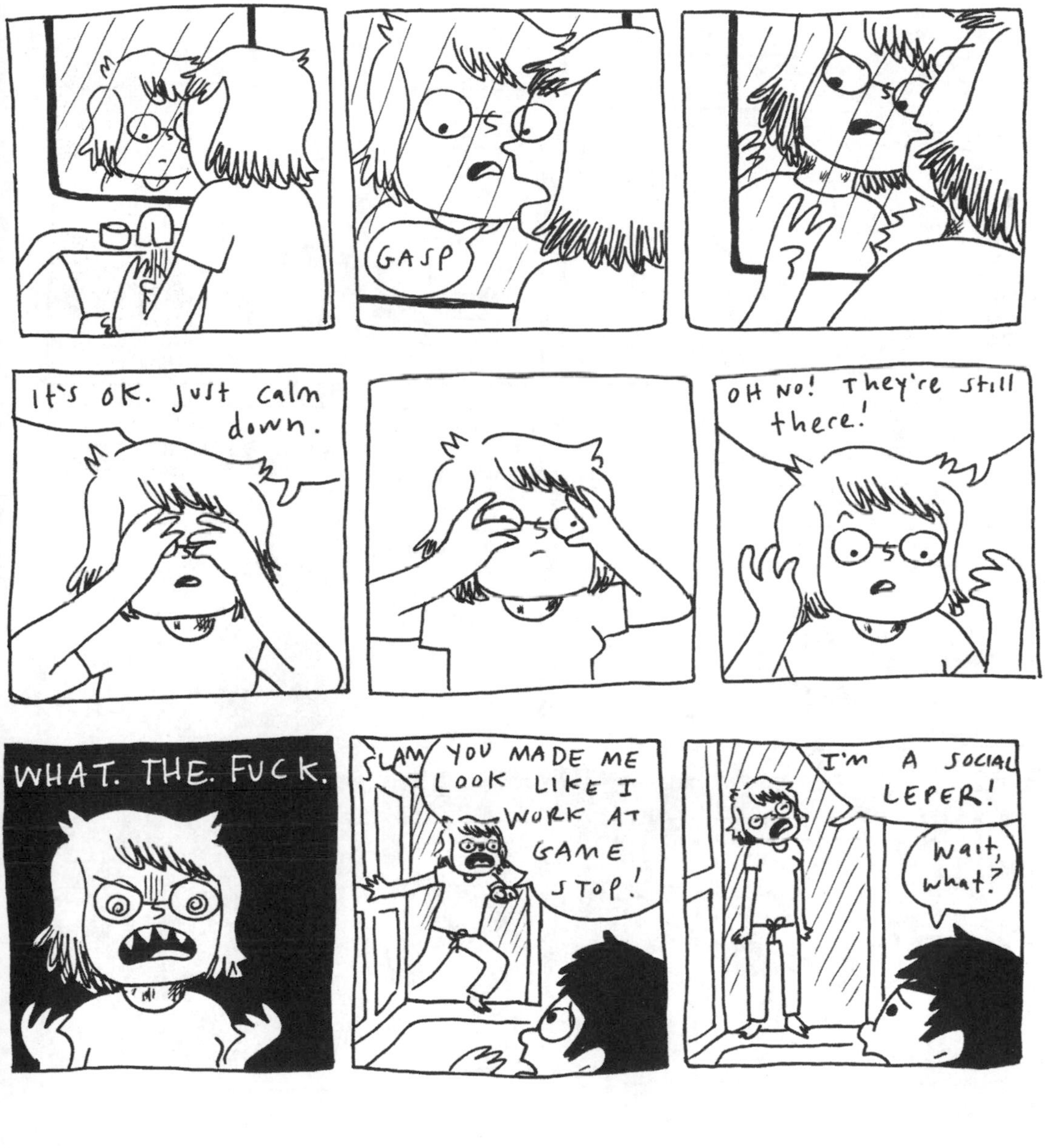
GASP
It's OK. Just calm down.
OH NO! They're still there!
WHAT. THE. FUCK.
SLAM
YOU MADE ME LOOK LIKE I WORK AT GAME STOP!
I'M A SOCIAL LEPER!
Wait, what?

Dark Days

Lately I've had this habit of falling asleep on the couch while it's light out

then waking up to a house that's pitch black

I lay in the dark thinking about how depressing it is

I wish I had "the clapper"

CLAP

CLAP

14

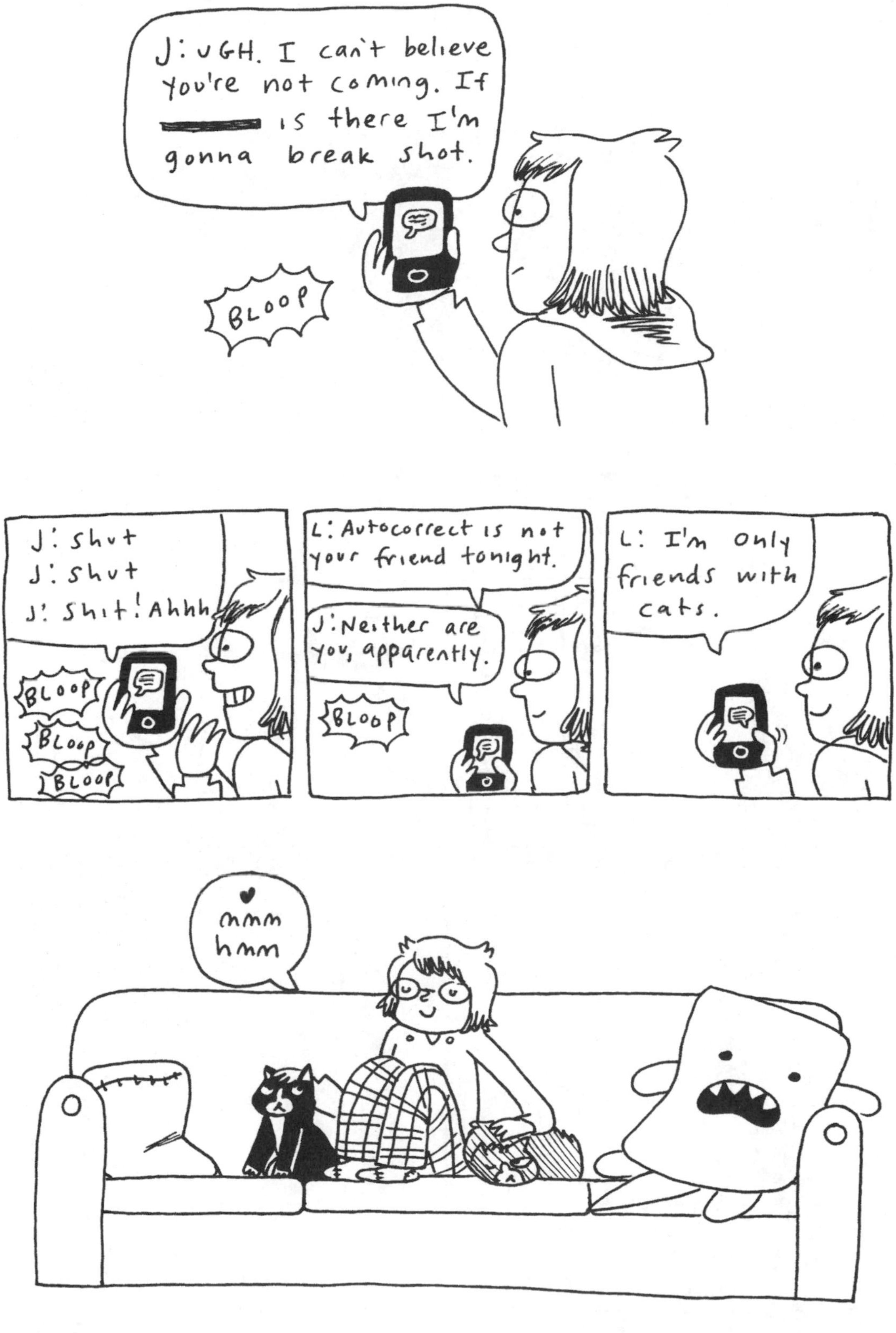
J: UGH. I can't believe you're not coming. If [redacted] is there I'm gonna break shot.
BLOOP
J: shut
J: shut
J: Shit! Ahhh
BLOOP
Bloop
BLOOP
L: Autocorrect is not your friend tonight.
J: Neither are you, apparently.
BLOOP
L: I'm only friends with cats.
mmm hmm

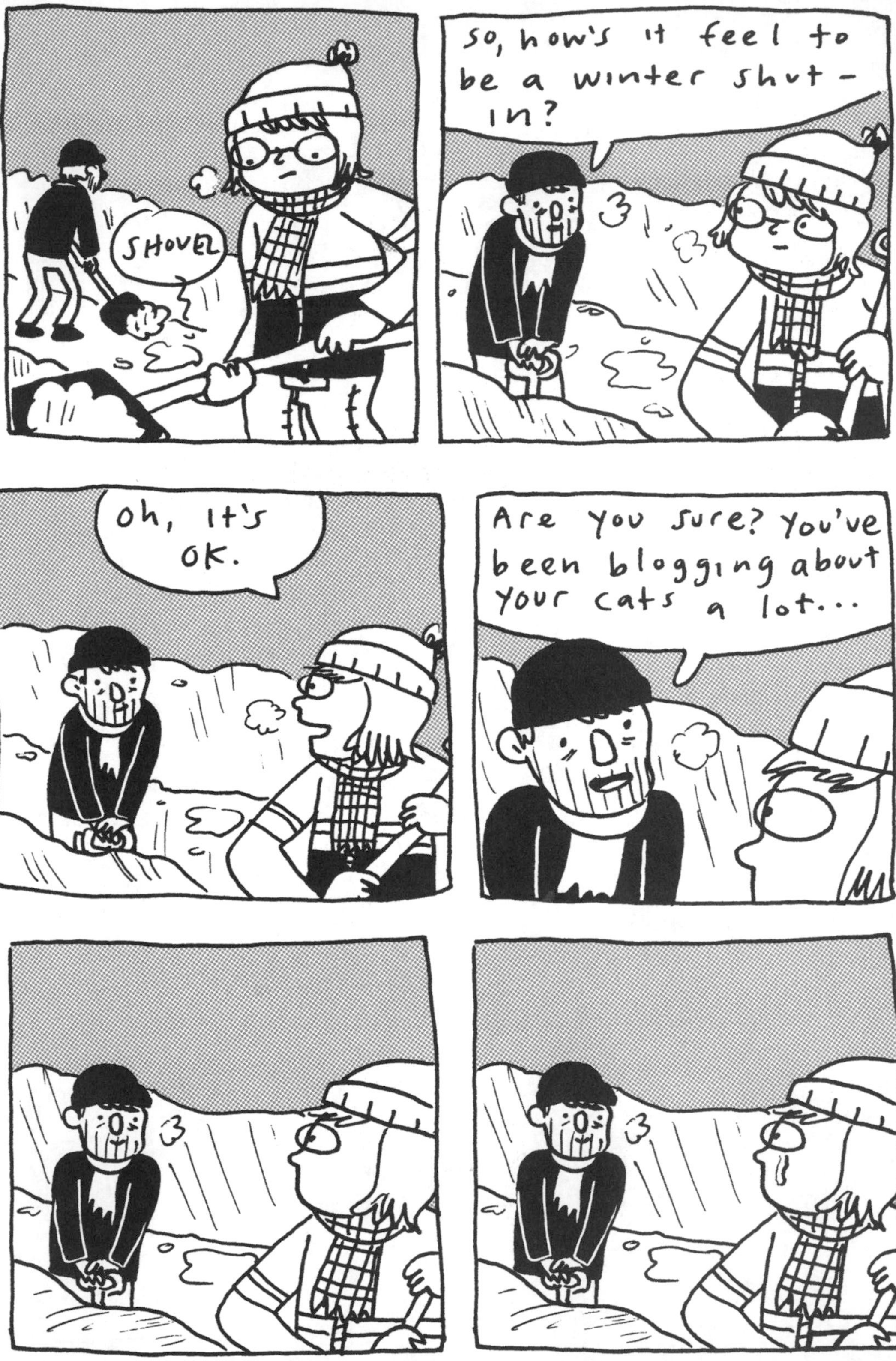
SHOVEL
So, how's it feel to be a winter shut-in?
Oh, it's OK.
Are you sure? You've been blogging about your cats a lot...

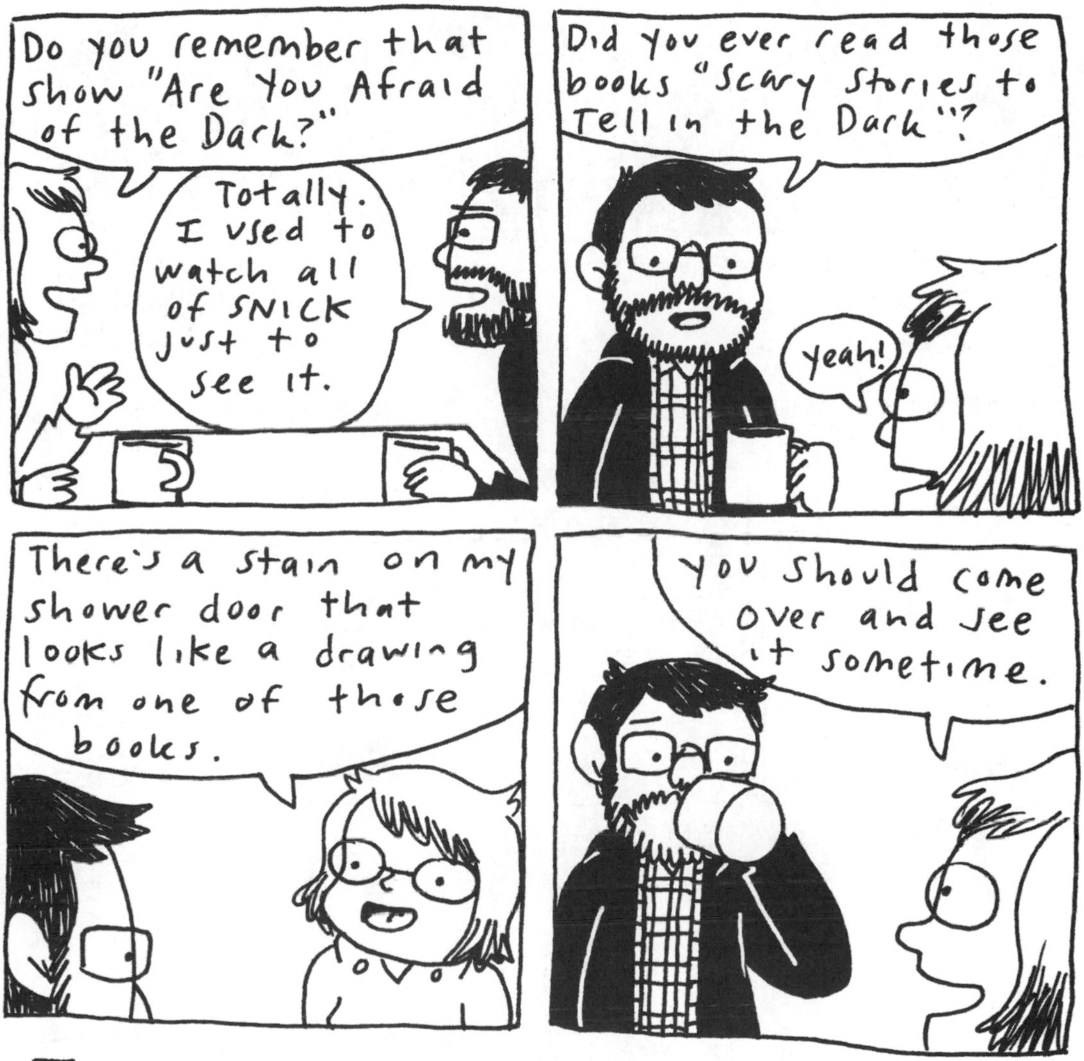
Do you remember that show "Are You Afraid of the Dark?"
Totally. I used to watch all of SNICK just to see it.
Did you ever read those books "Scary Stories to Tell in the Dark"?
yeah!
There's a stain on my shower door that looks like a drawing from one of those books.
You should come over and see it sometime.

I AM THE MASTER OF THE FLIRT.

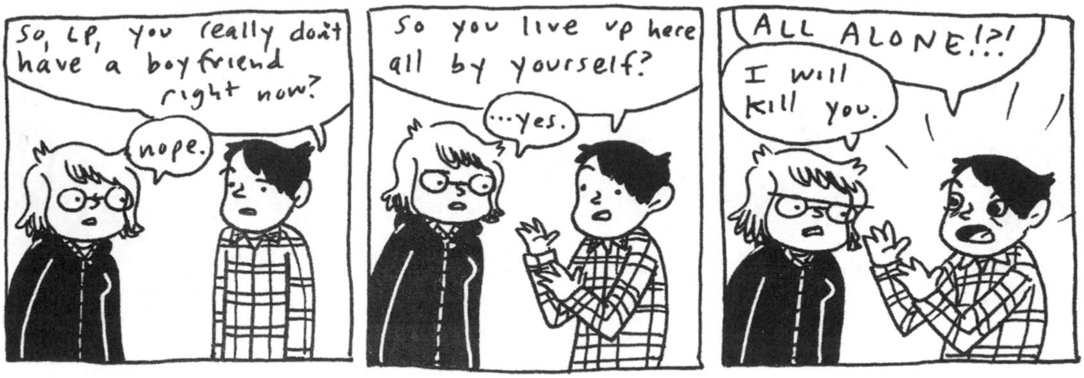
So, LP, you really don't have a boyfriend right now?
nope.
So you live up here all by yourself?
...yes.
ALL ALONE!?!
I will kill you.

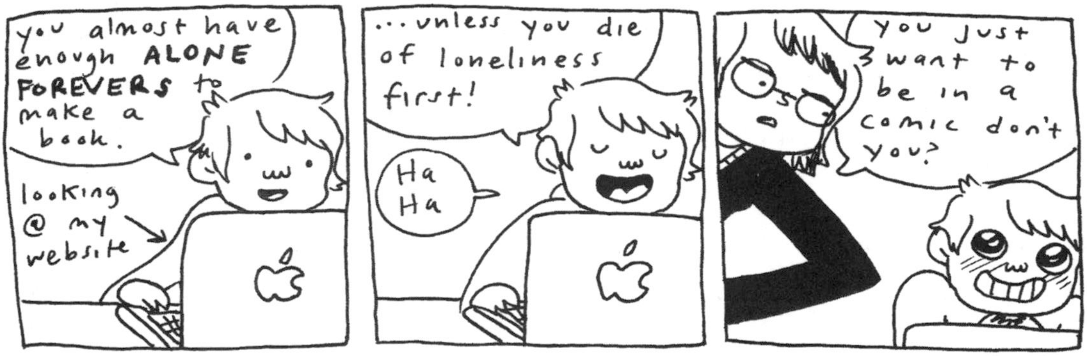
you almost have enough **ALONE FOREVERS** to make a book.
looking @ my website
...unless you die of loneliness first!
Ha Ha
You just want to be in a comic don't you?

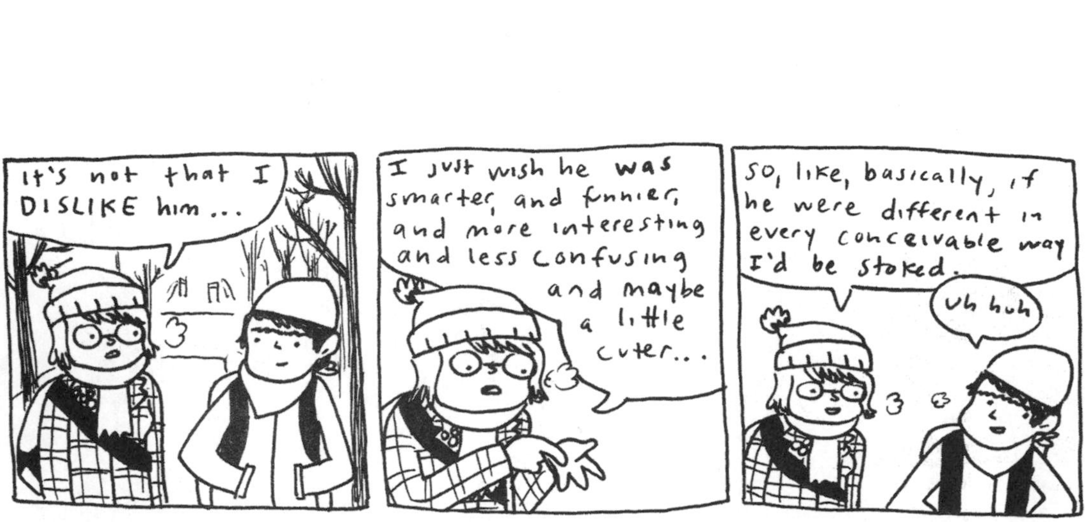
It's not that I DISLIKE him...
I just wish he **was** smarter, and funnier, and more interesting and less confusing and maybe a little cuter...
So, like, basically, if he were different in every conceivable way I'd be stoked.
Uh huh

I was agressively pursued by a guy in a somewhat popular punk band, he didn't live near me, and I wasn't attracted to him, but his tenacity and wit won me over

Despite the distance, it was nice to go bed at night feeling crushed out on someone

But soon communication became sparse and my view of the situation was starting to get tainted

TXT unreturned

email unanswered

NO NEW messages

empty P.O. Box

flirtation gave way to frustration

He would pop-up from time to time to try to reignite our "crush"

Hey, I've been busy but I'm thinking of you.

and any conversation I'd try to have on the subject of my annoyance was unsatisfactory

It is hard to say Bye when someone asks you to give them a chance

He was really cool at first

remember?

But part of growing up is learning to remove yourself from undesirable situations

Yeah, for about 2 seconds

oh, c'mon!

AH! SHUT UP!

SLAM

Book of love

Because when you're not on the same page

It's best to just tear that page out

RIP

and move on

TOSS

Man, all the cute Lemuria fan girls went home already.
what? I'm not cute enough for you?
That's not what I meant!
you're cute! ... is that really an option?
Ha
No

Terms of endearment

Have you heard from that ok cupid guy?
the fat vegan?
... I guess?
No. I guess he hates me for some reason.
And you call him "the Fat Vegan"?
well, not to his FACE

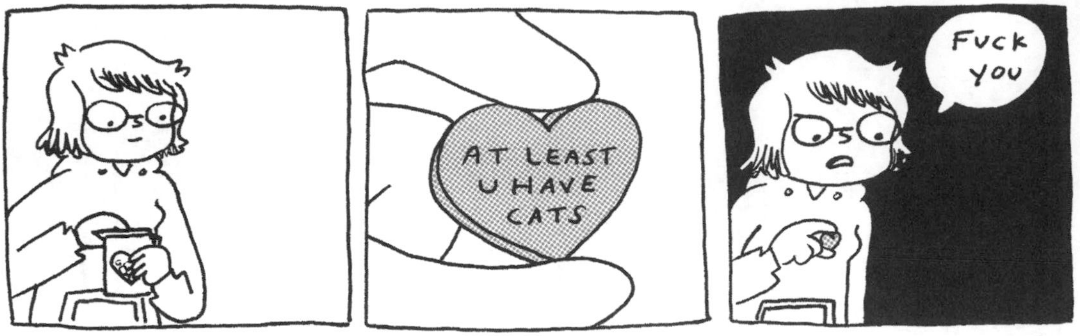
AT LEAST
U HAVE
CATS
Fuck you

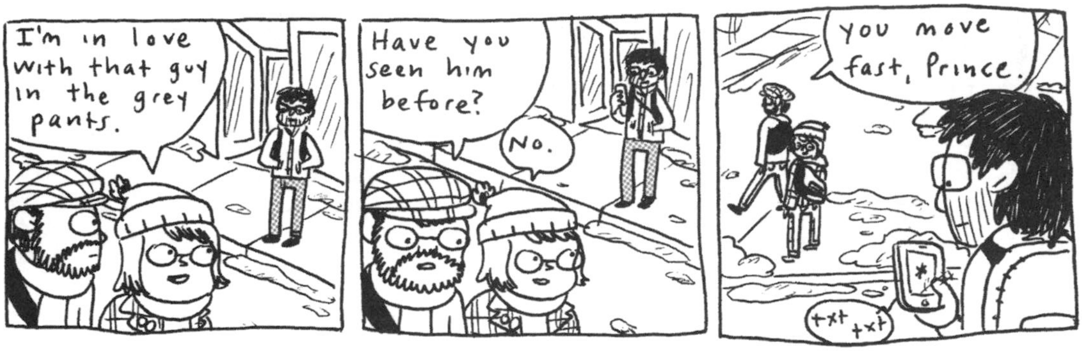
I'm in love with that guy in the grey pants.
Have you seen him before?
No.
you move fast, Prince.
*
txt txt

* there's a weird girl making eyes at me...

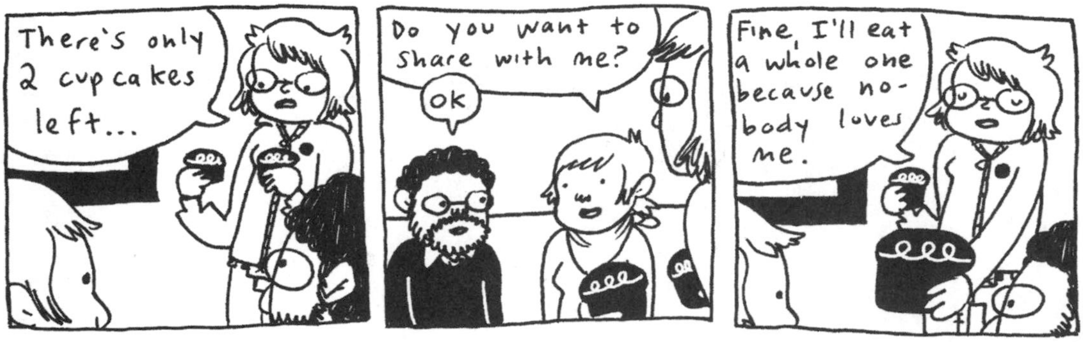
There's only 2 cupcakes left...
Do you want to share with me?
ok
Fine I'll eat a whole one because no-body loves me.

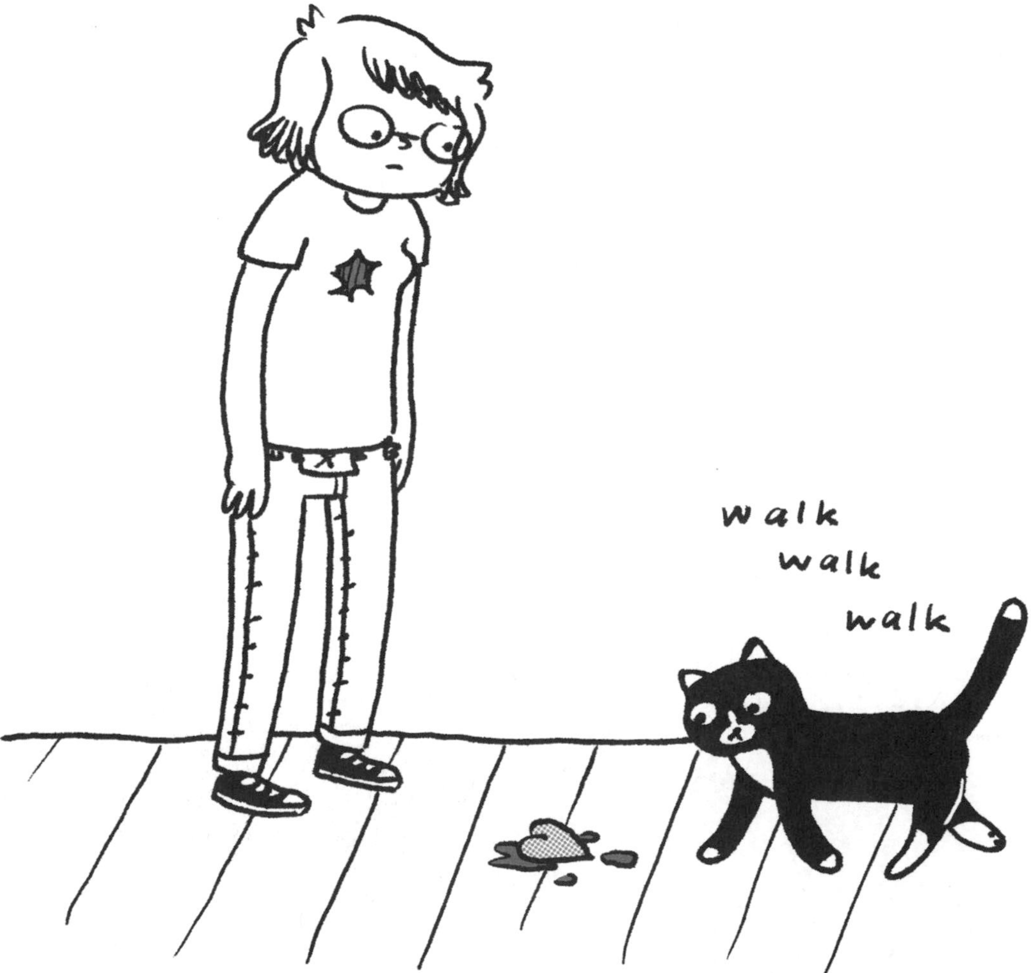
walk
walk
walk

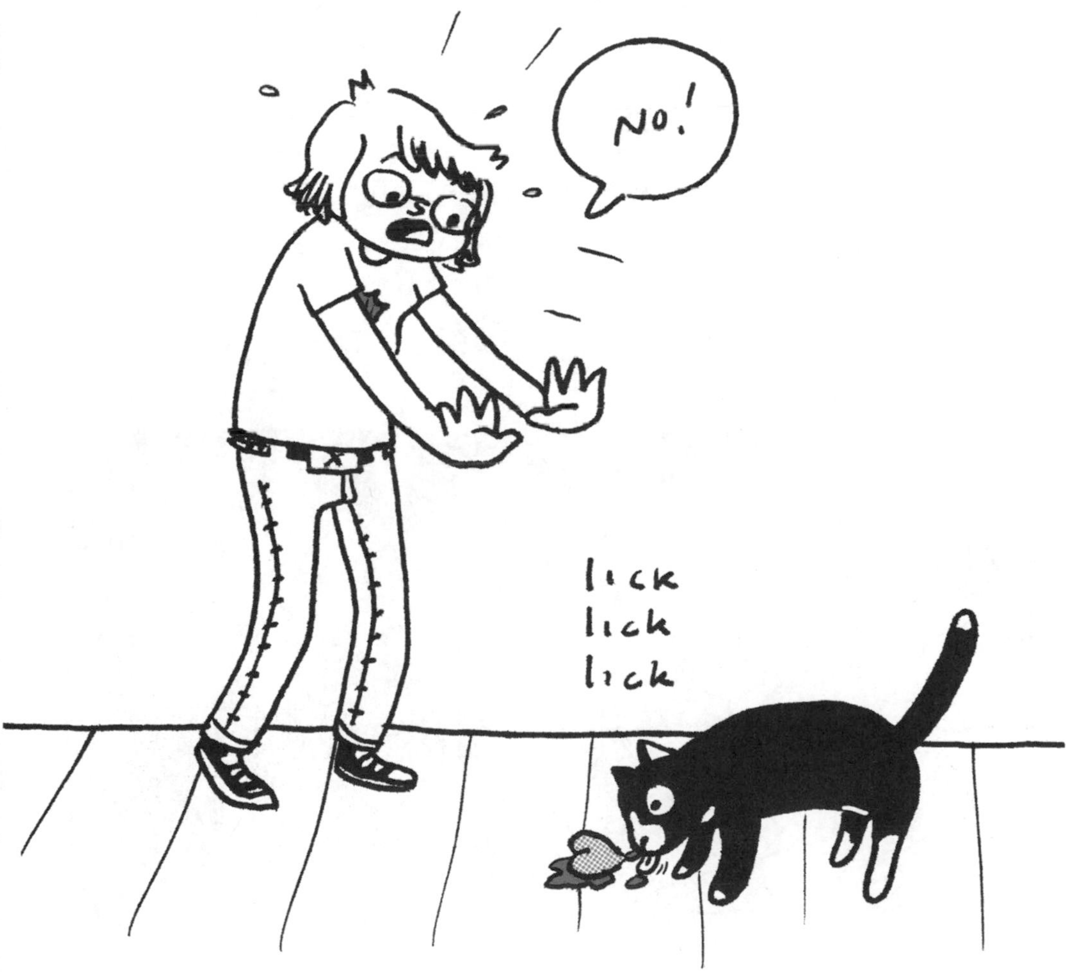
No!
lick
lick
lick

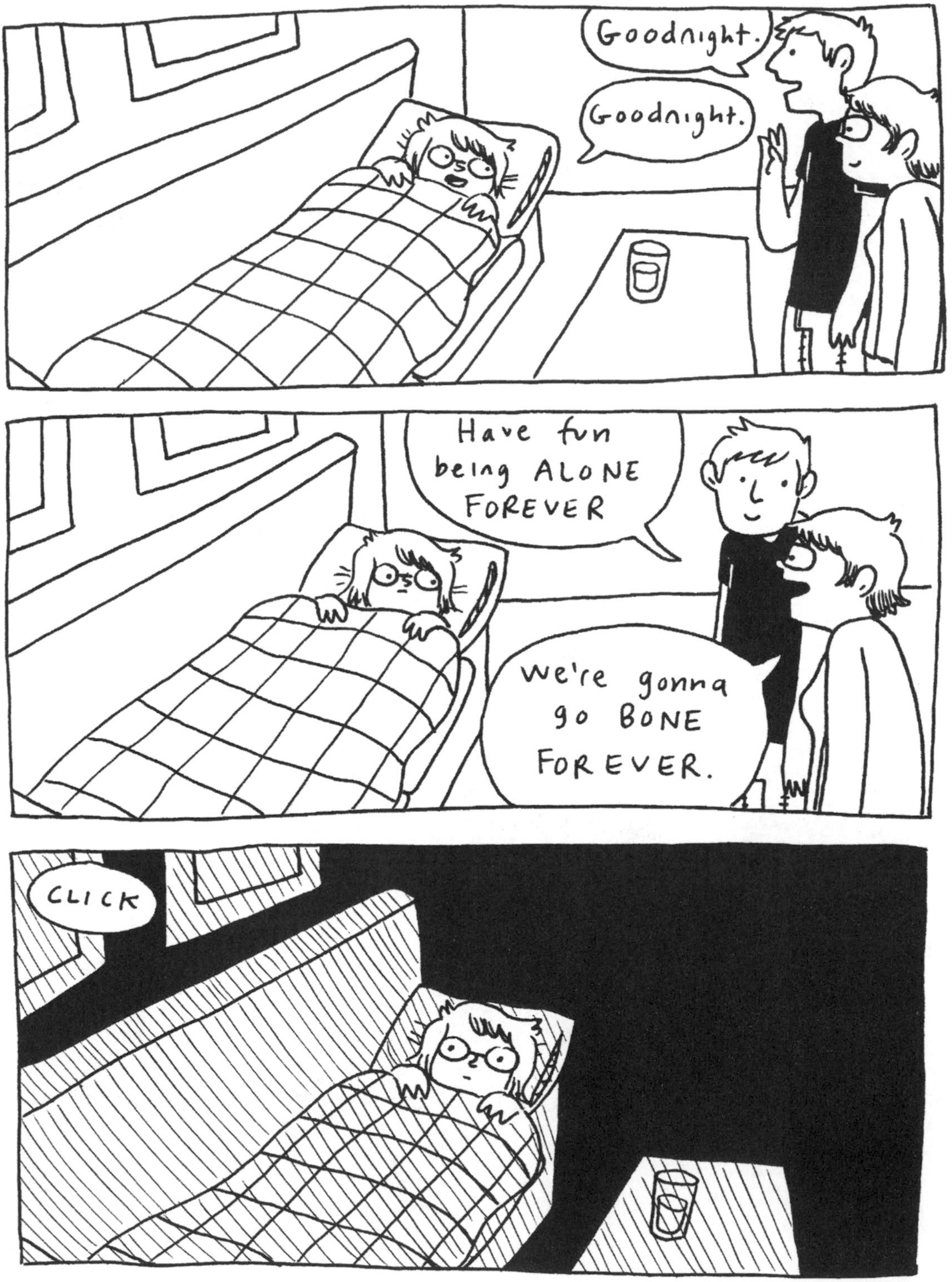

Goodnight.
Goodnight.
Have fun being ALONE FOREVER
We're gonna go BONE FOREVER.
CLICK

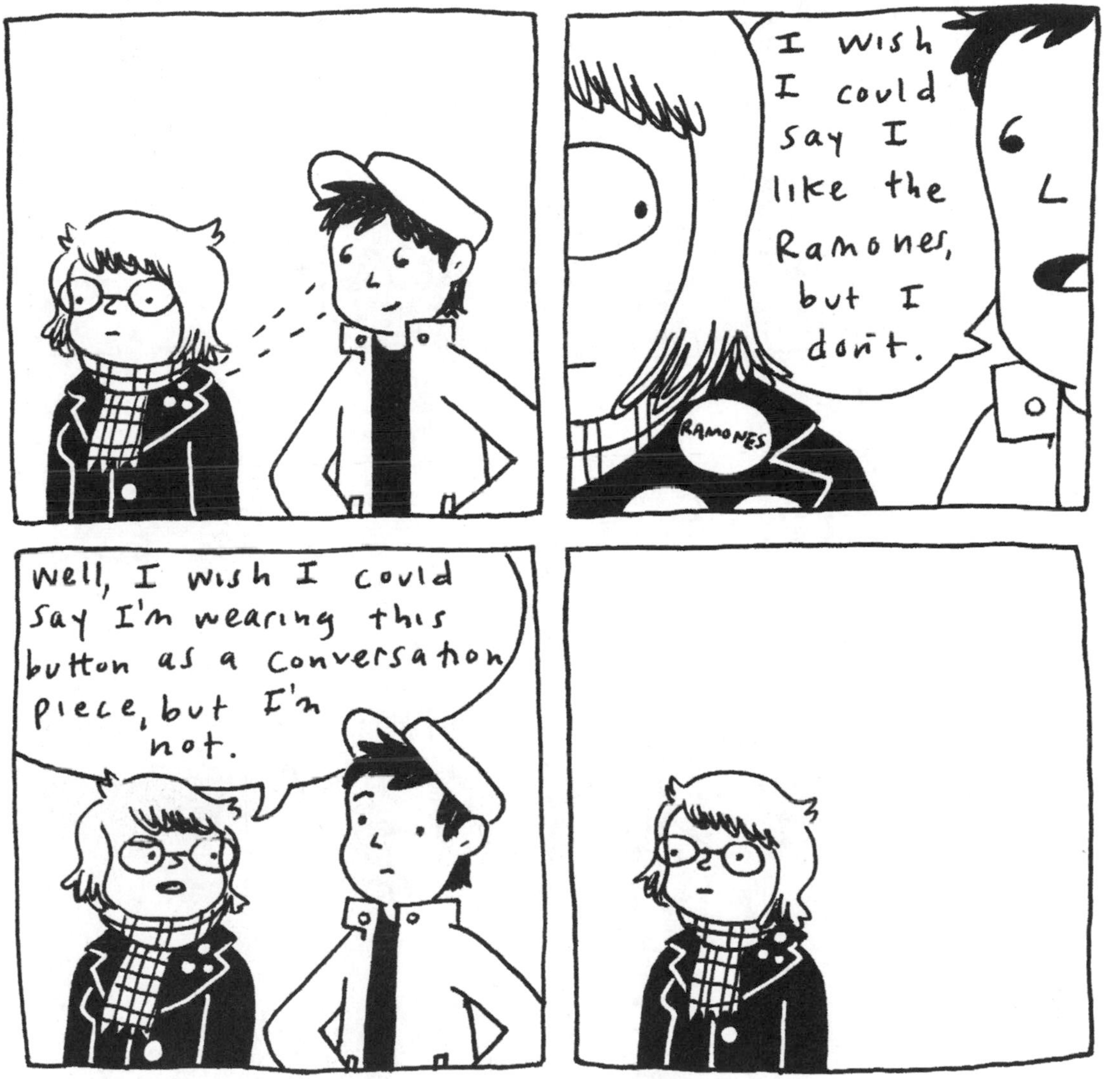
I wish I could say I like the Ramones, but I don't.
RAMONES
Well, I wish I could say I'm wearing this button as a conversation piece, but I'm not.

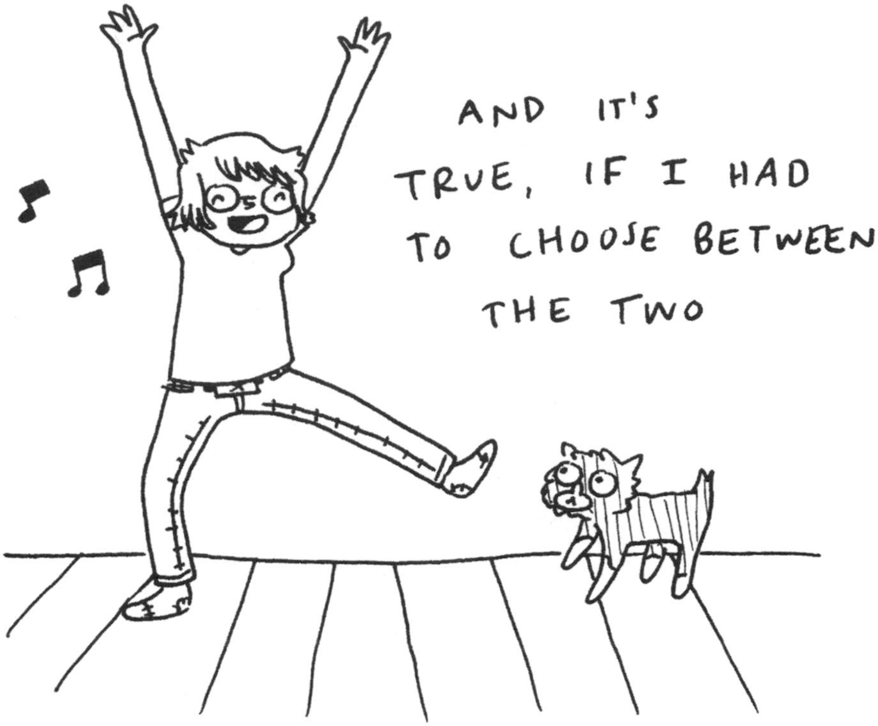
AND IT'S TRUE, IF I HAD TO CHOOSE BETWEEN THE TWO

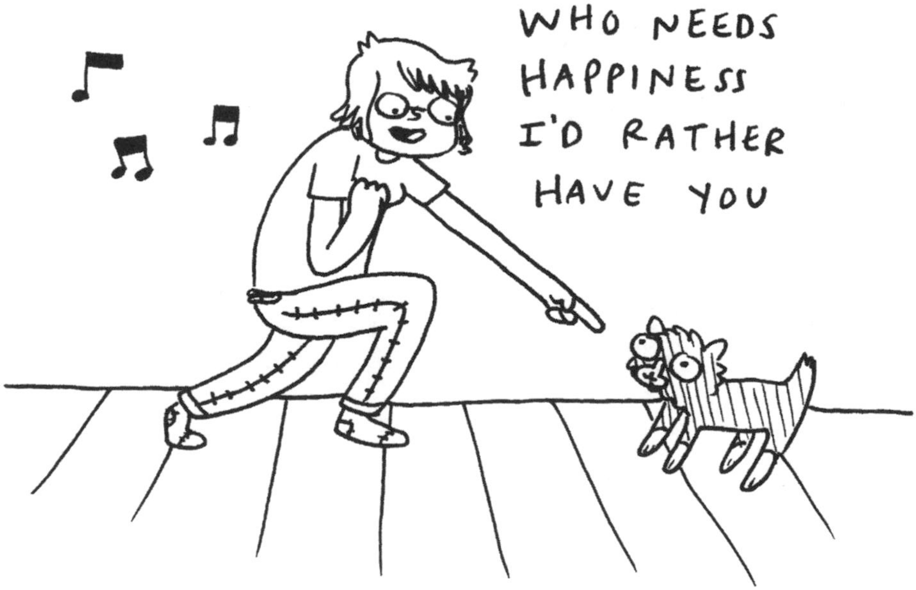
WHO NEEDS HAPPINESS I'D RATHER HAVE YOU

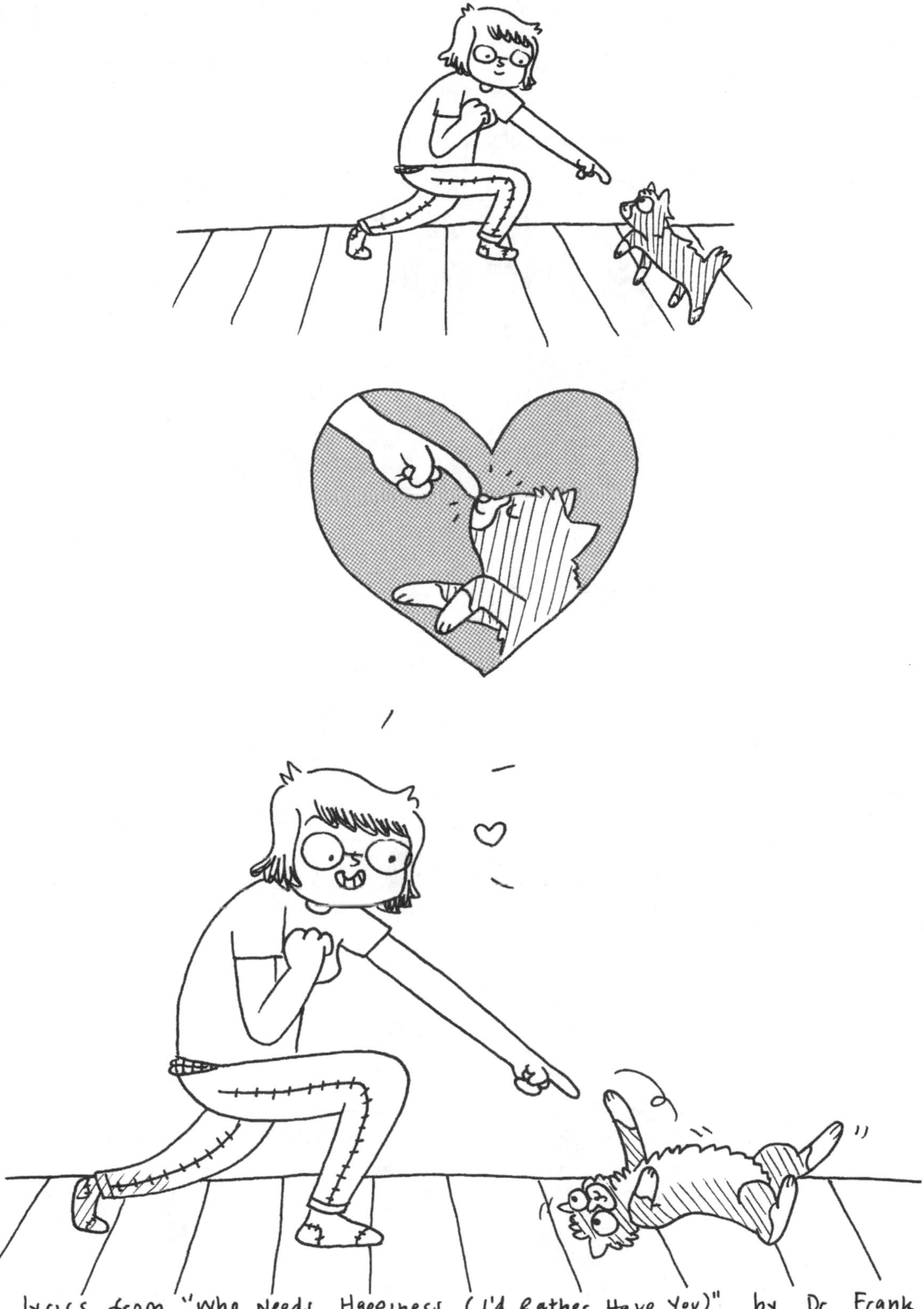

lyrics from "Who Needs Happiness (I'd Rather Have You)" by Dr. Frank

@ the Lemuria show

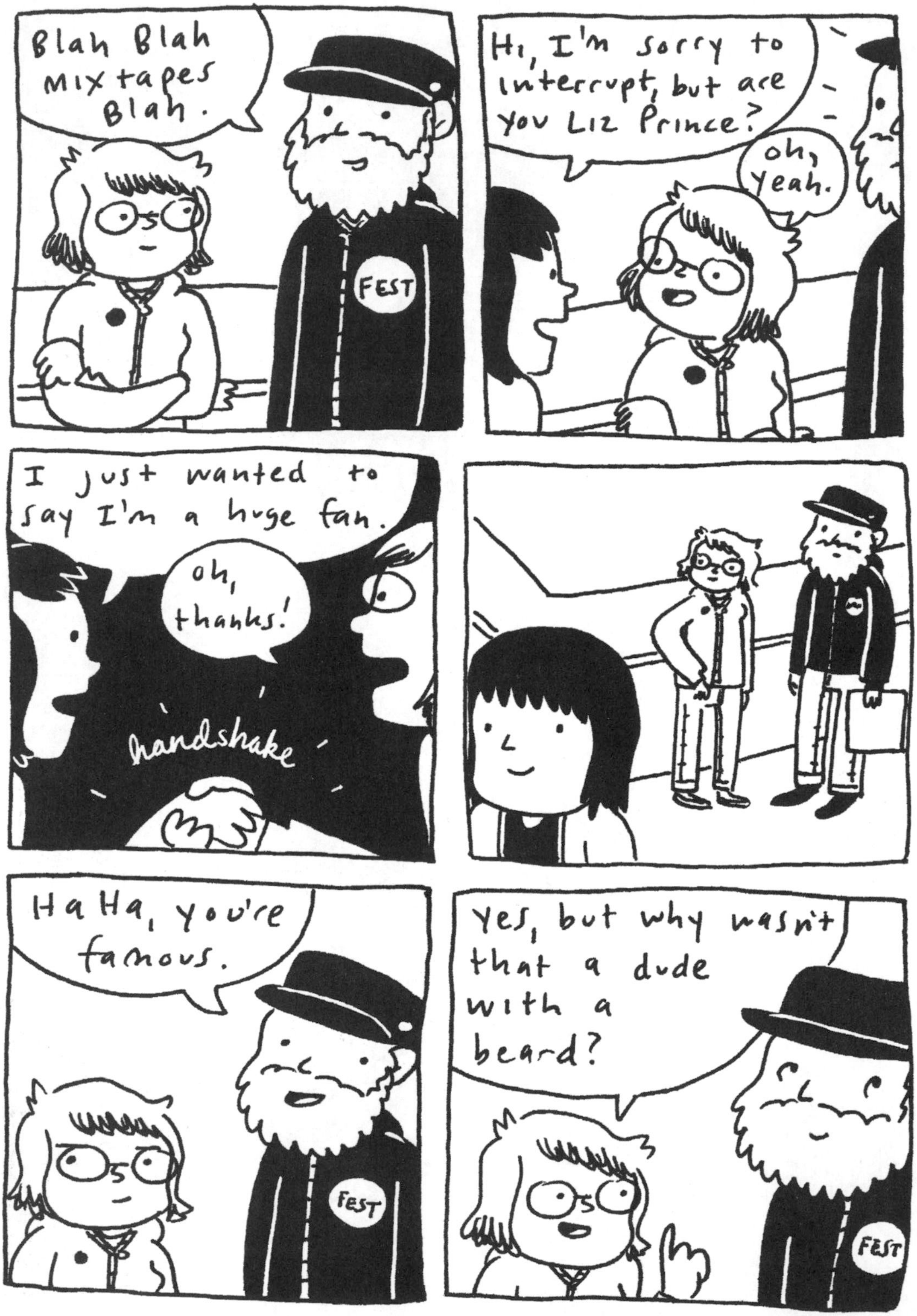
Blah Blah Mixtapes Blah.
FEST
Hi, I'm sorry to interrupt, but are you Liz Prince?
oh, yeah.
I just wanted to say I'm a huge fan.
oh, thanks!
handshake
HaHa, you're famous.
FEST
Yes, but why wasn't that a dude with a beard?
FEST

@ the Art Store

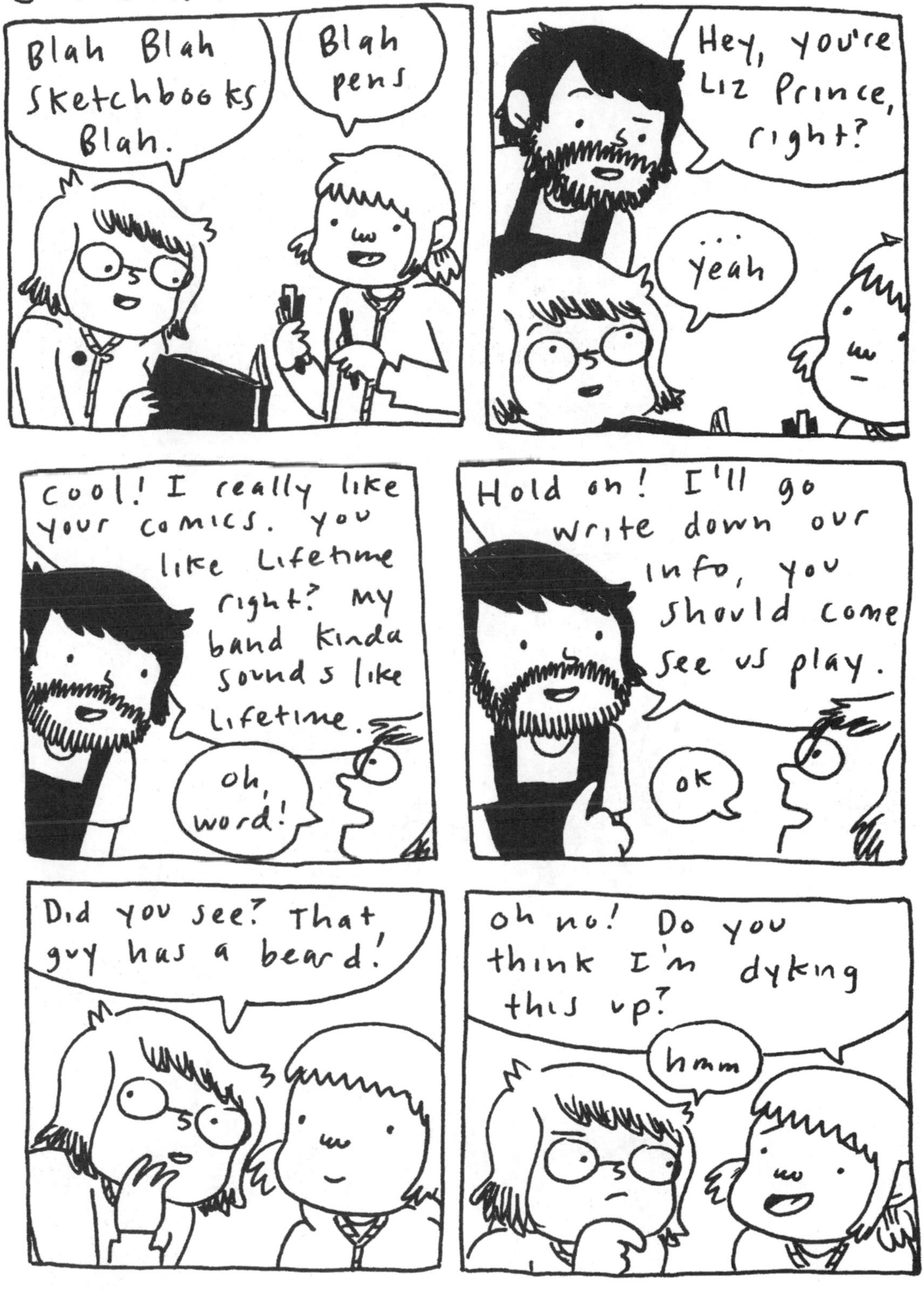

Blah Blah Sketchbooks Blah.
Blah pens
Hey, you're Liz Prince, right?
... yeah
Cool! I really like your comics. You like Lifetime right? My band kinda sounds like Lifetime.
oh, word!
Hold on! I'll go write down our info, you should come see us play.
ok
Did you see? That guy has a beard!
oh no! Do you think I'm dyking this up?
hmm

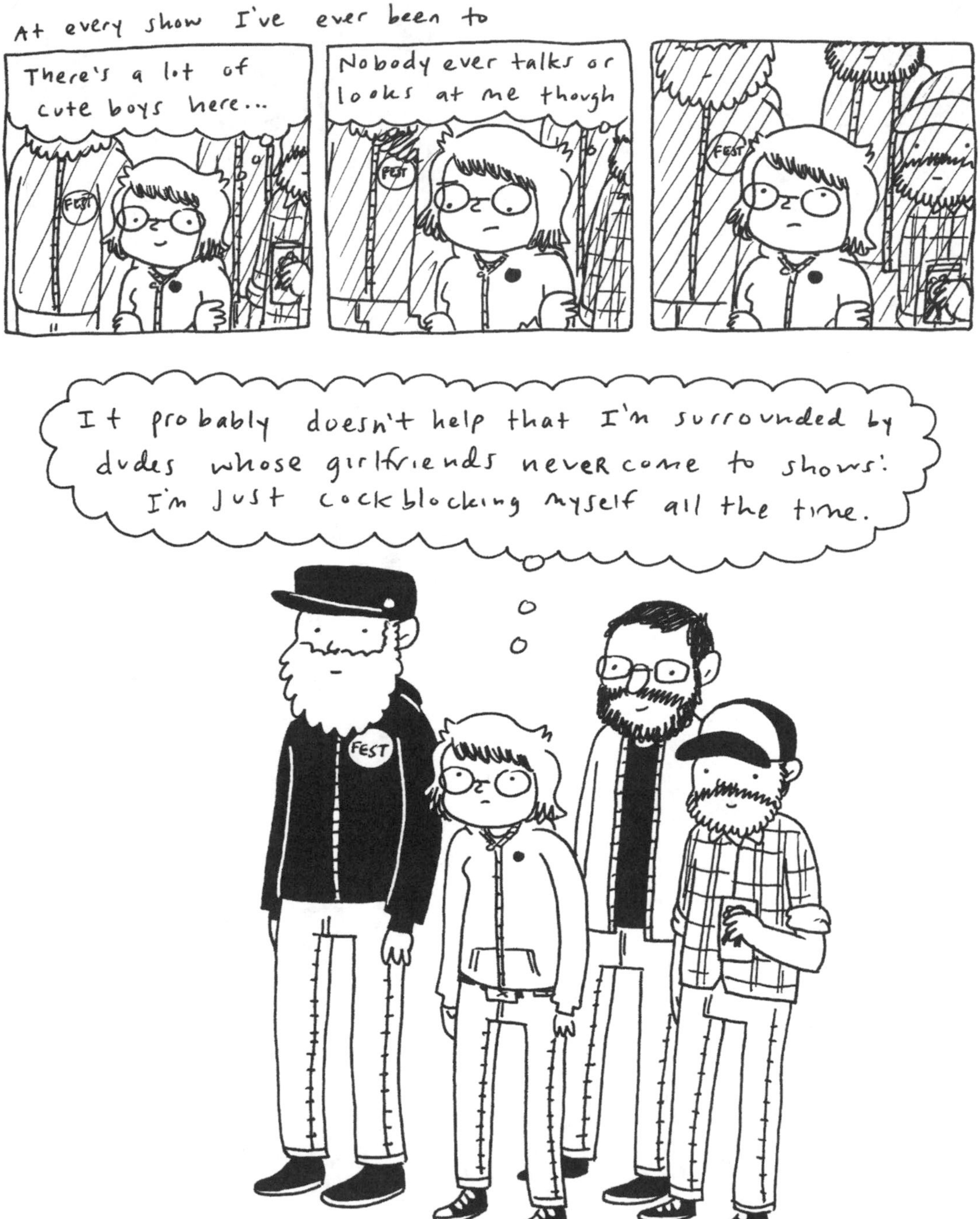
At every show I've ever been to
There's a lot of cute boys here...
FEST
Nobody ever talks or looks at me though
FEST
FEST
It probably doesn't help that I'm surrounded by dudes whose girlfriends never come to shows: I'm just cockblocking myself all the time.
FEST

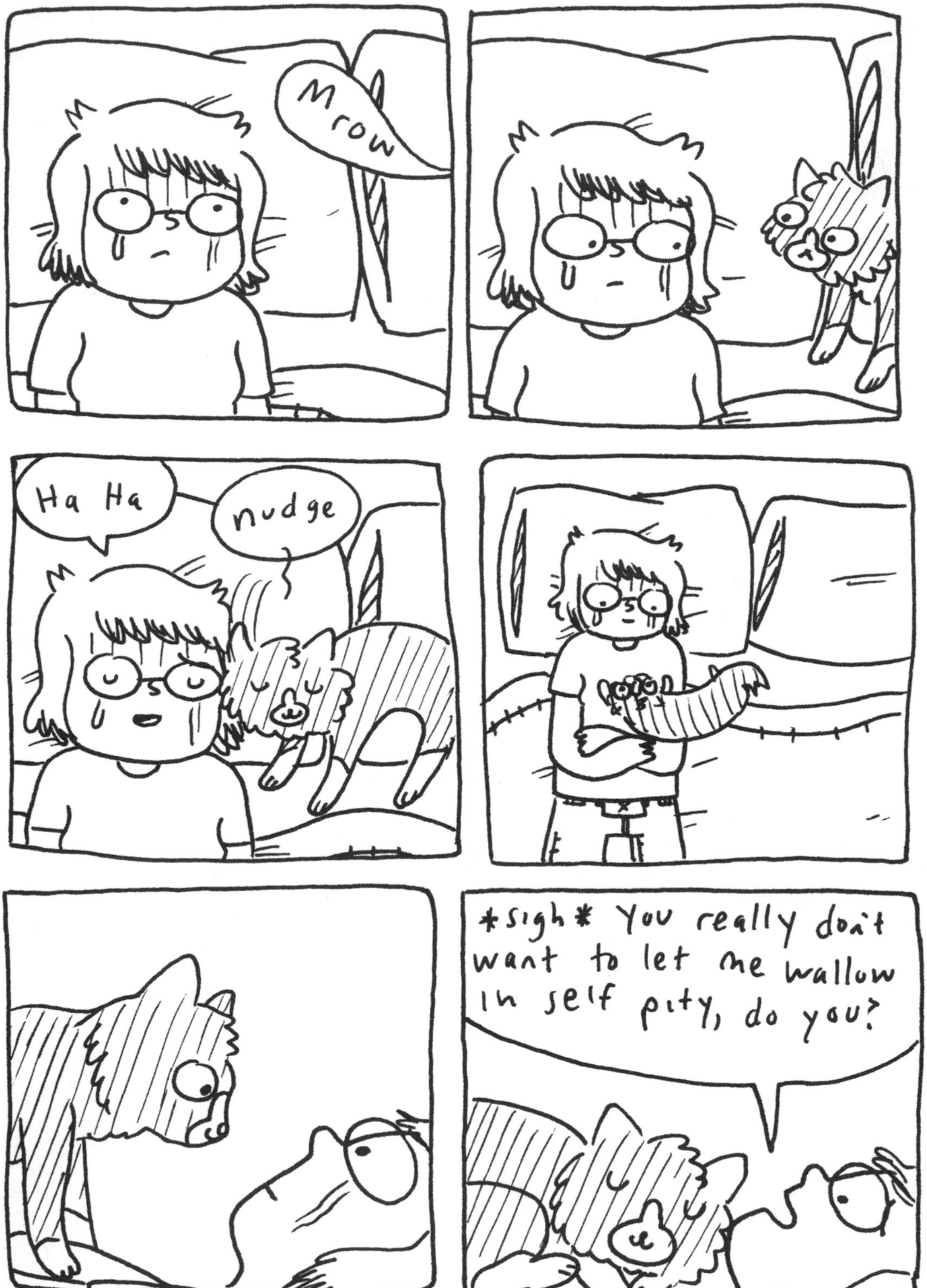
Mrow
Ha Ha
nudge
sigh You really don't want to let me wallow in self pity, do you?

PURRRRRRR

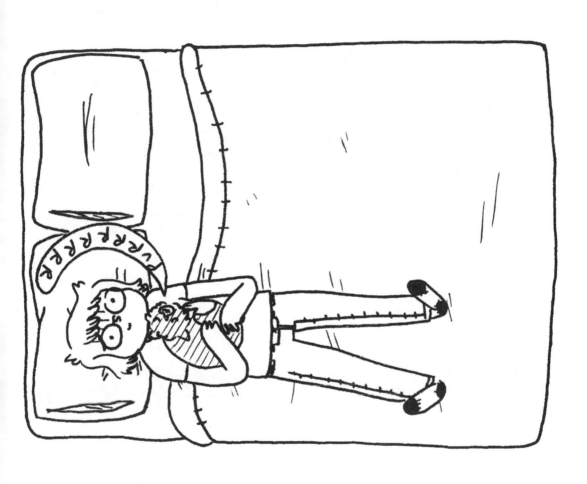

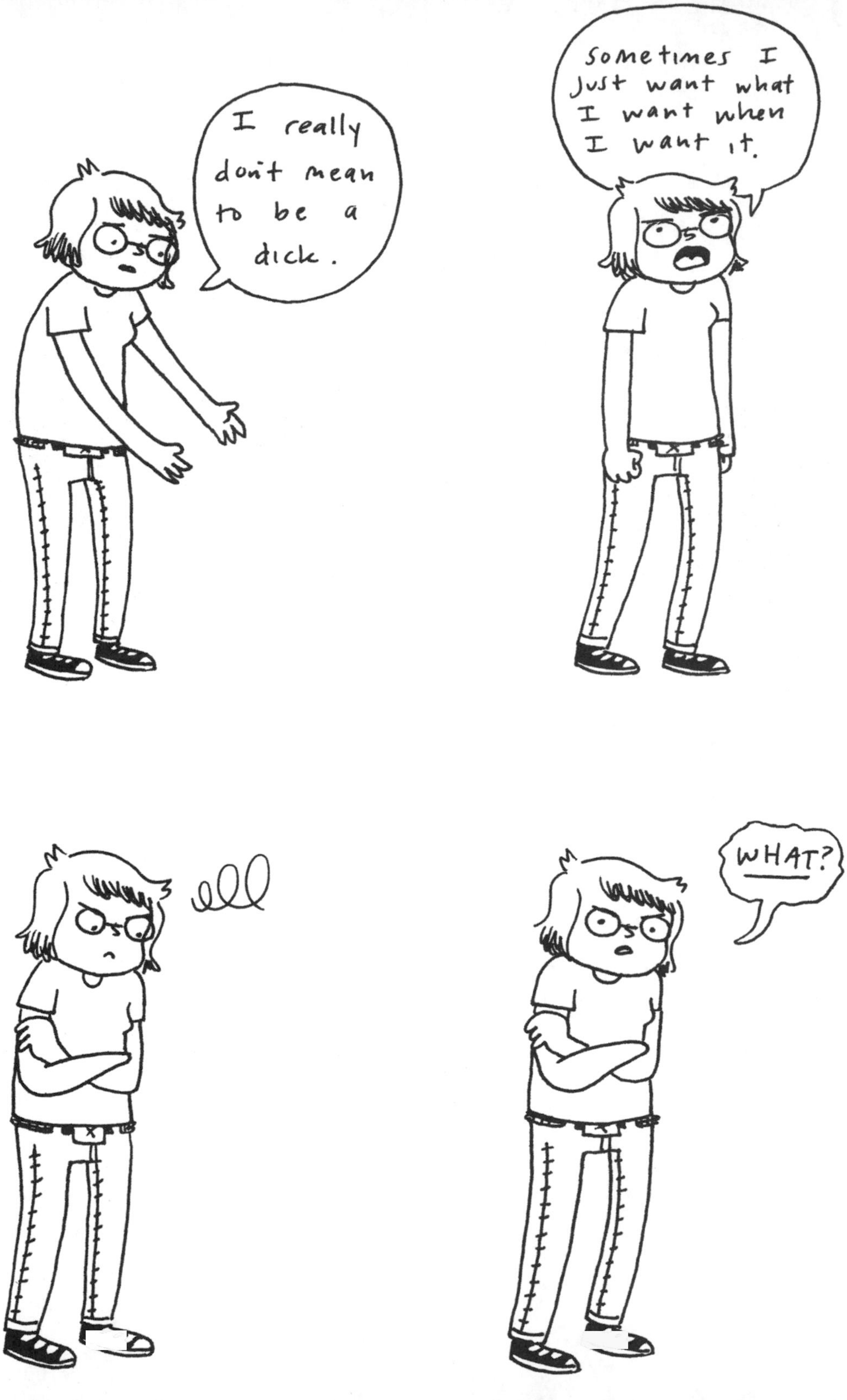
I really don't mean to be a dick.
Sometimes I just want what I want when I want it.
WHAT?

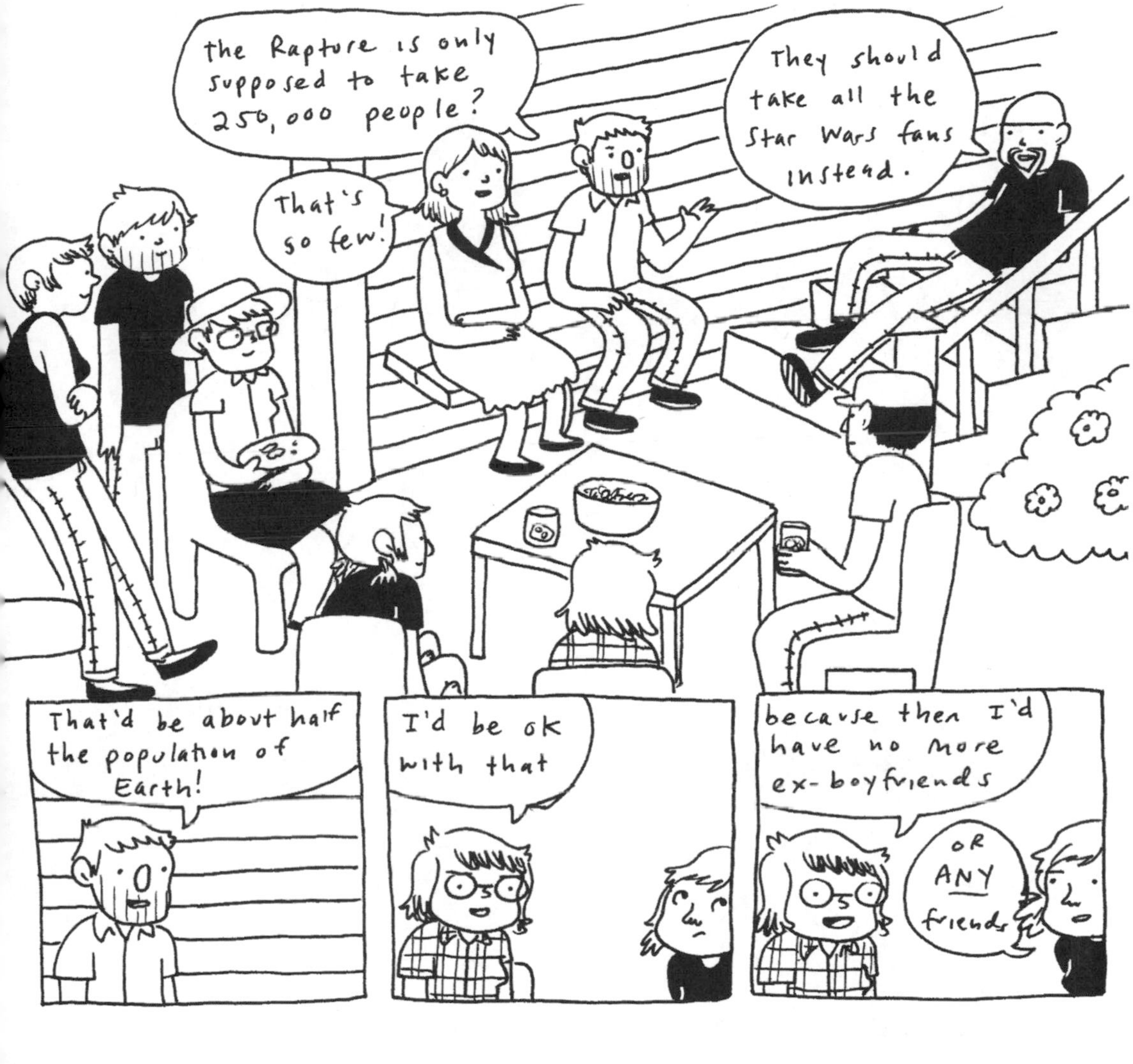
the Rapture is only supposed to take 250,000 people?
That's so few!
They should take all the Star Wars fans instead.
That'd be about half the population of Earth!
I'd be ok with that
because then I'd have no more ex-boyfriends
OR ANY friends

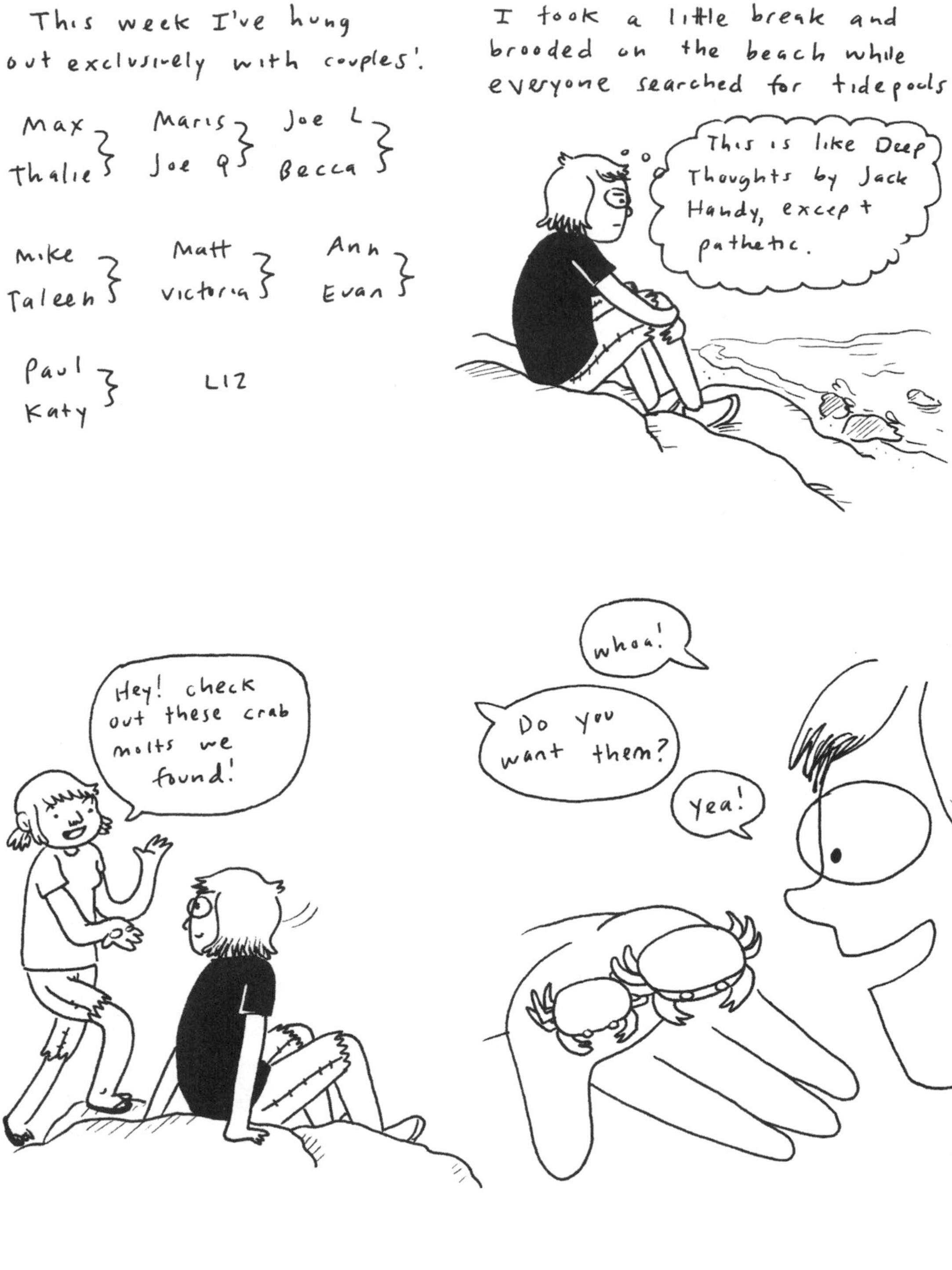
This week I've hung out exclusively with couples!
Max } Thalie
Maris } Joe Q
Joe L } Becca
Mike } Taleen
Matt } Victoria
Ann } Evan
Paul } Katy
LIZ
I took a little break and brooded on the beach while everyone searched for tidepools
This is like Deep Thoughts by Jack Handy, except pathetic.
Hey! check out these crab molts we found!
whoa!
Do you want them?
yea!

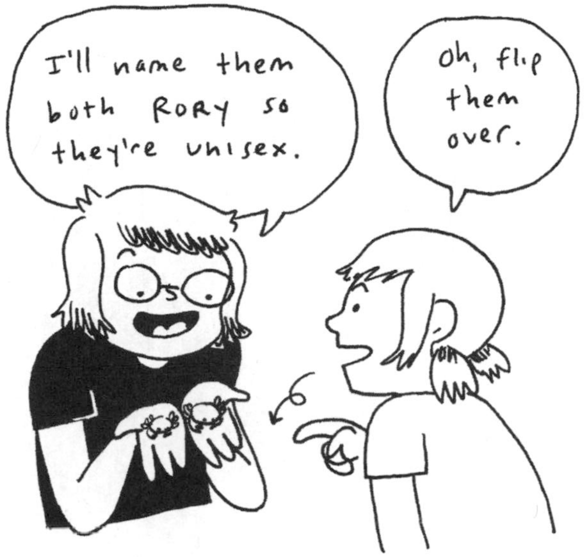
I'll name them both RORY so they're unisex.
Oh, flip them over.

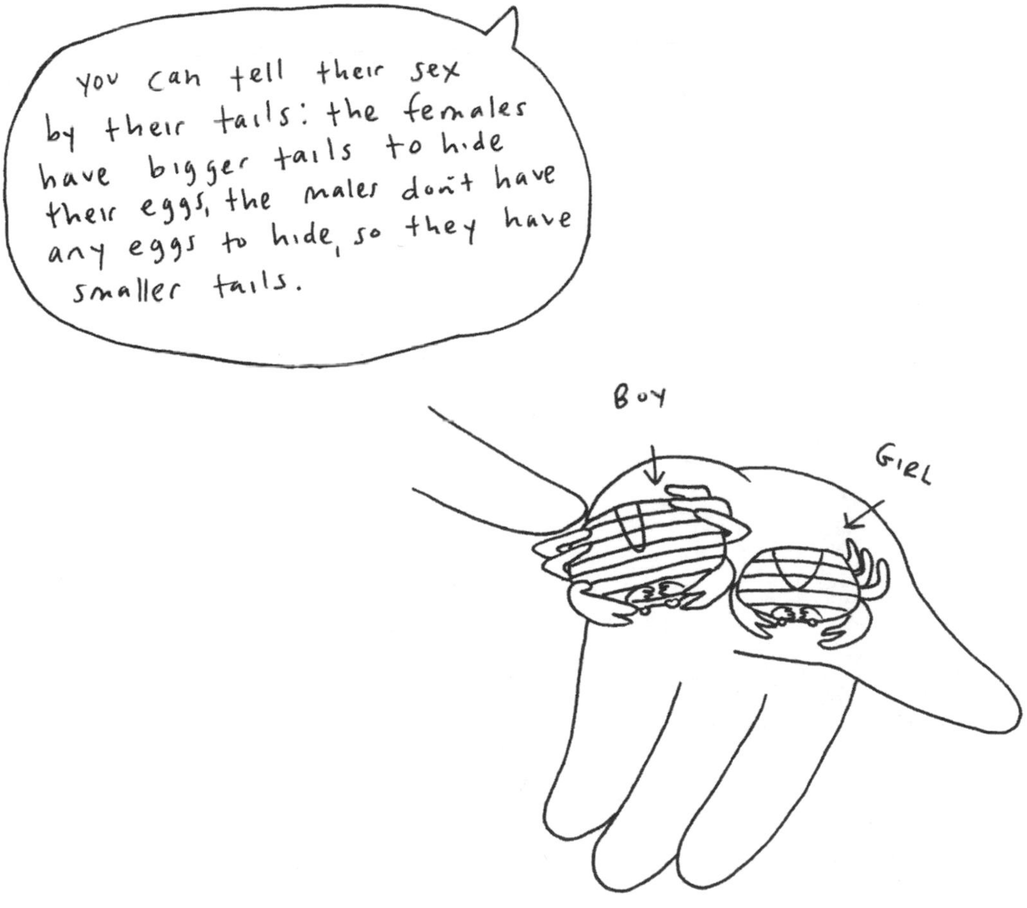
You can tell their sex by their tails: the females have bigger tails to hide their eggs, the males don't have any eggs to hide, so they have smaller tails.
BOY
GIRL

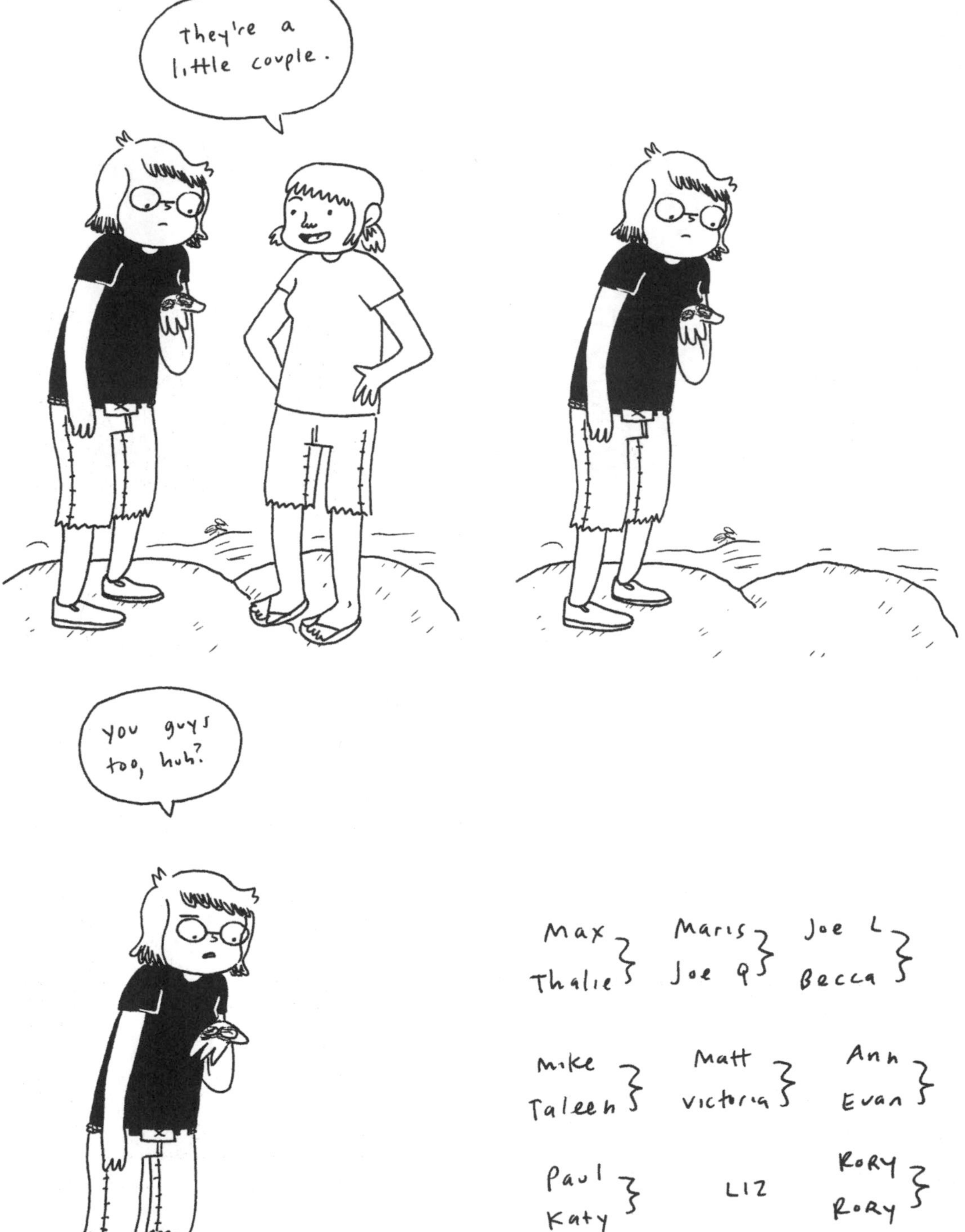
they're a little couple.
you guys too, huh?
Max
Thalie
Maris
Joe Q
Joe L
Becca
Mike
Taleen
Matt
victoria
Ann
Evan
Paul
Katy
LIZ
RORY
RORY

Telling someone you have a crush on them via text message is so fucking nerve wracking

Duh huh
I, like, like LIKE you, y'know?
TXT TXT TXT
Minute 1
WAIT WAIT WAIT
Minute 2
heh heh
WAIT WAIT
Minute 2.5
oh god
Minute 3
what am I doing?
Minute 3.5
He hates me
Minute 4
DESPAIR
SLUMP
Minute 6
TWITCH
BZZT
WOOOOW. I have a crush on you too, obvs.
GLEE

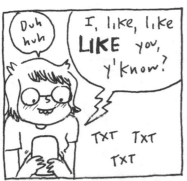

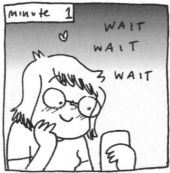

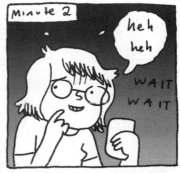

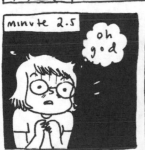

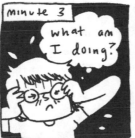

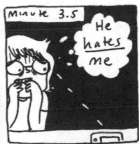

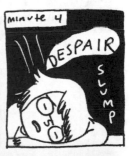

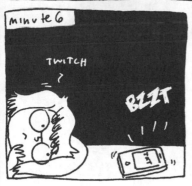

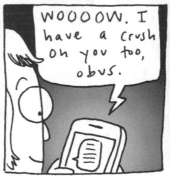

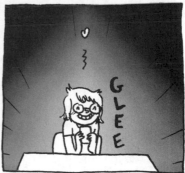

The one where Liz gets hit on at a party

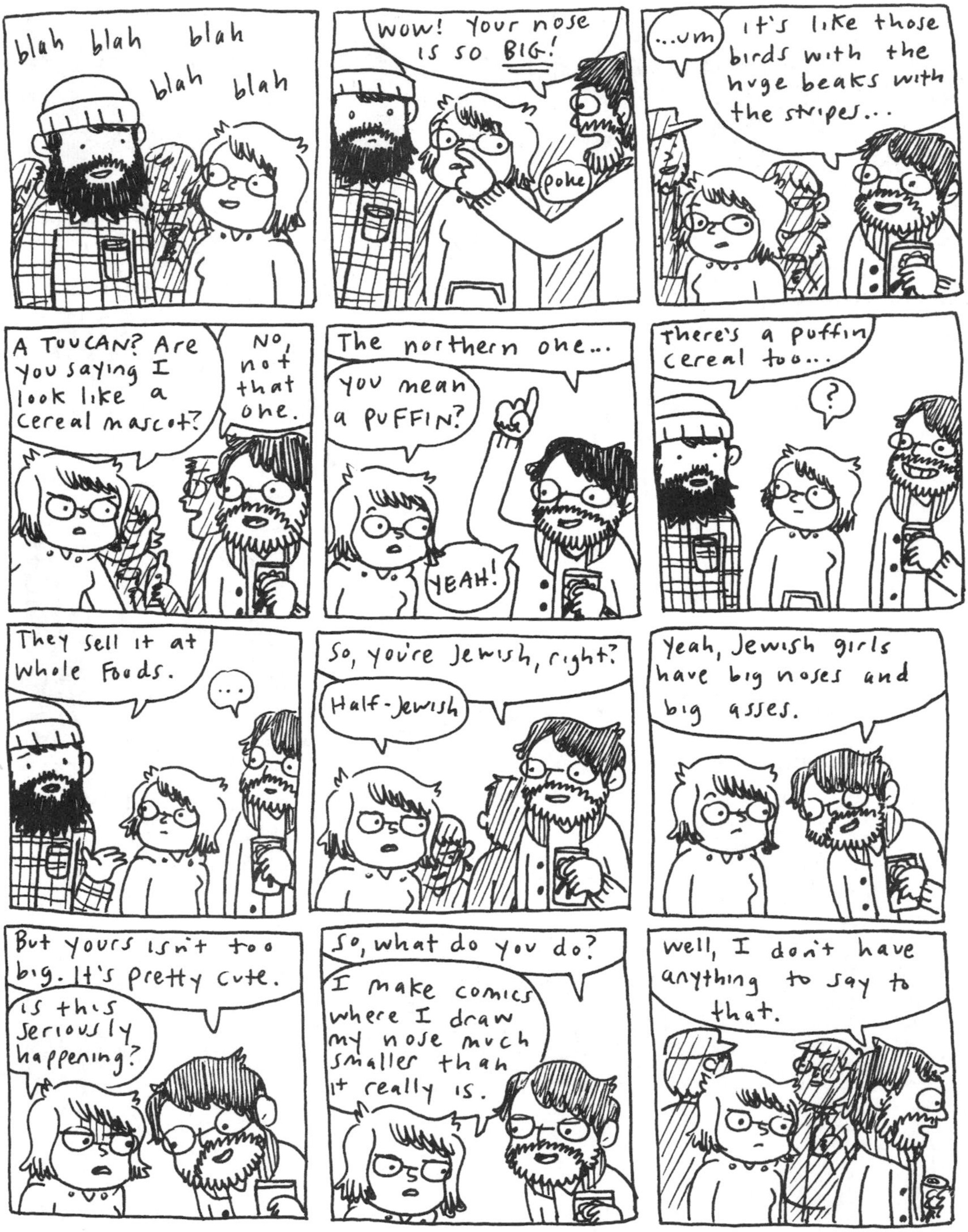

blah blah blah
blah blah
WOW! Your nose is so BIG!
poke
...um
It's like those birds with the huge beaks with the stripes...
A TOUCAN? Are you saying I look like a cereal mascot?
No, not that one.
The northern one...
You mean a PUFFIN?
YEAH!
There's a puffin cereal too...
?
They sell it at Whole Foods.
...
So, you're Jewish, right?
Half-Jewish
Yeah, Jewish girls have big noses and big asses.
But yours isn't too big. It's pretty cute.
Is this seriously happening?
So, what do you do?
I make comics where I draw my nose much smaller than it really is.
Well, I don't have anything to say to that.

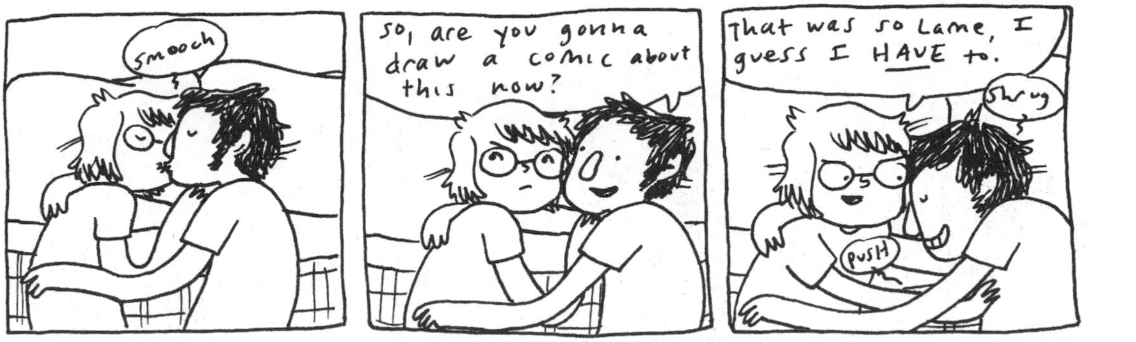
smooch
so, are you gonna draw a comic about this now?
That was so Lame, I guess I HAVE to.
Shrug
PUSH

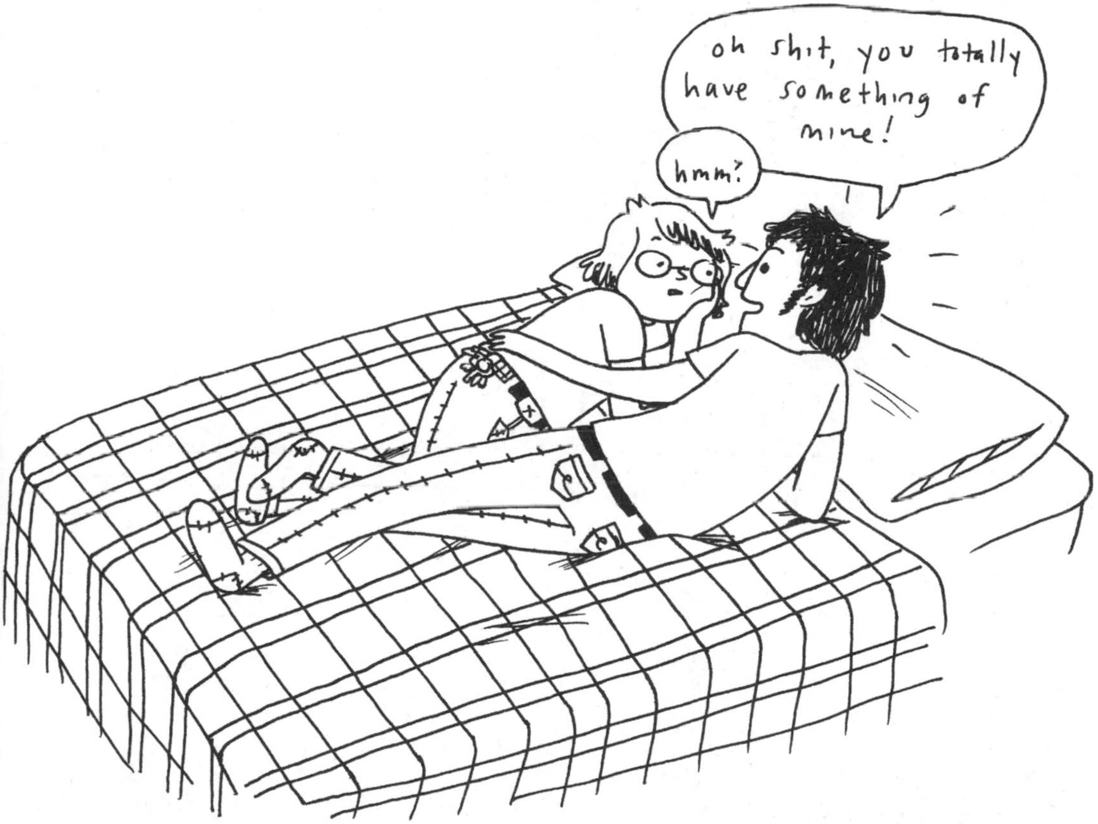
oh shit, you totally have something of mine!
hmm?

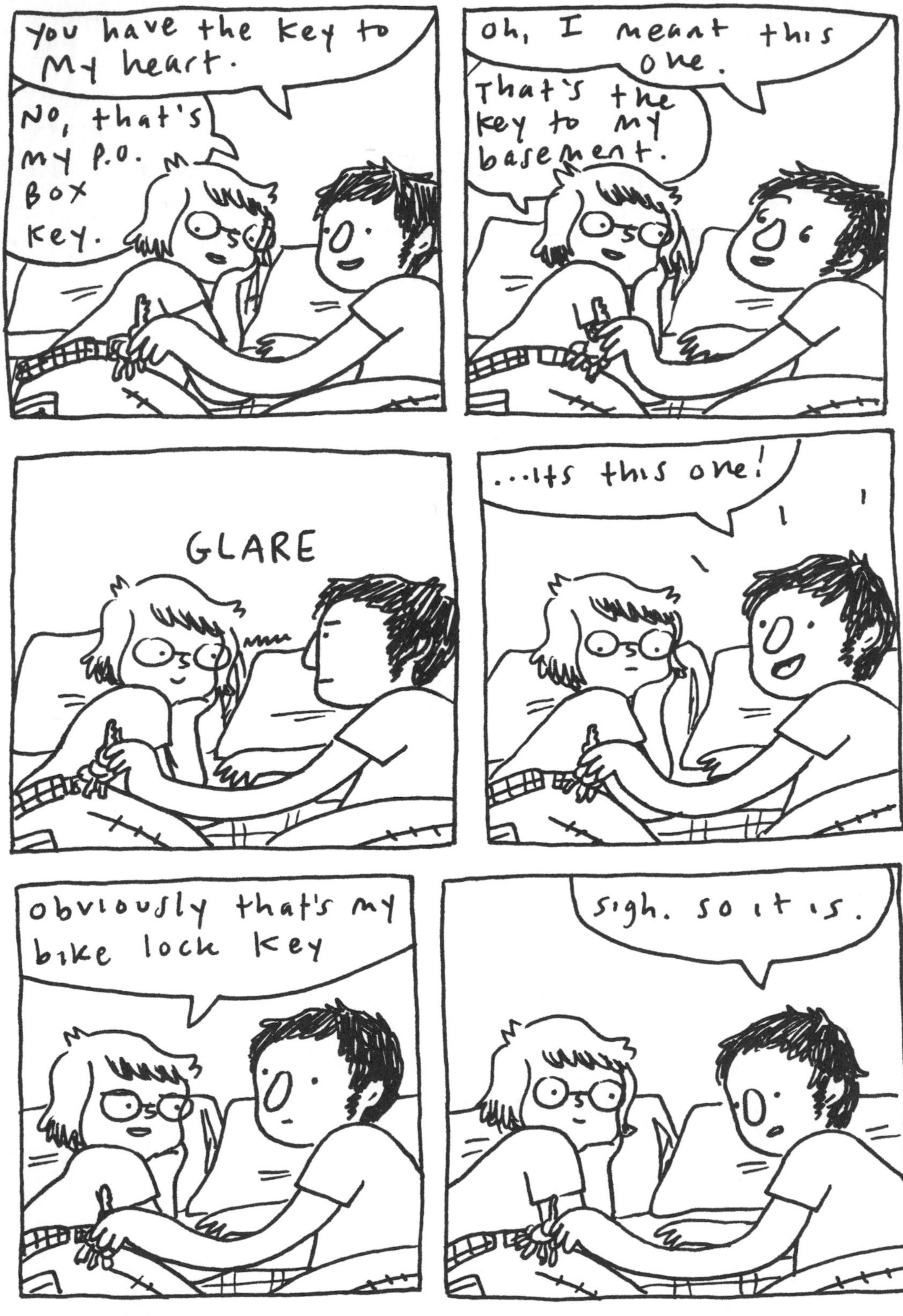
you have the key to My heart.
No, that's my P.O. Box key.
oh, I meant this one.
That's the key to my basement.
GLARE
...its this one!
obviously that's my bike lock key
sigh. so it is.

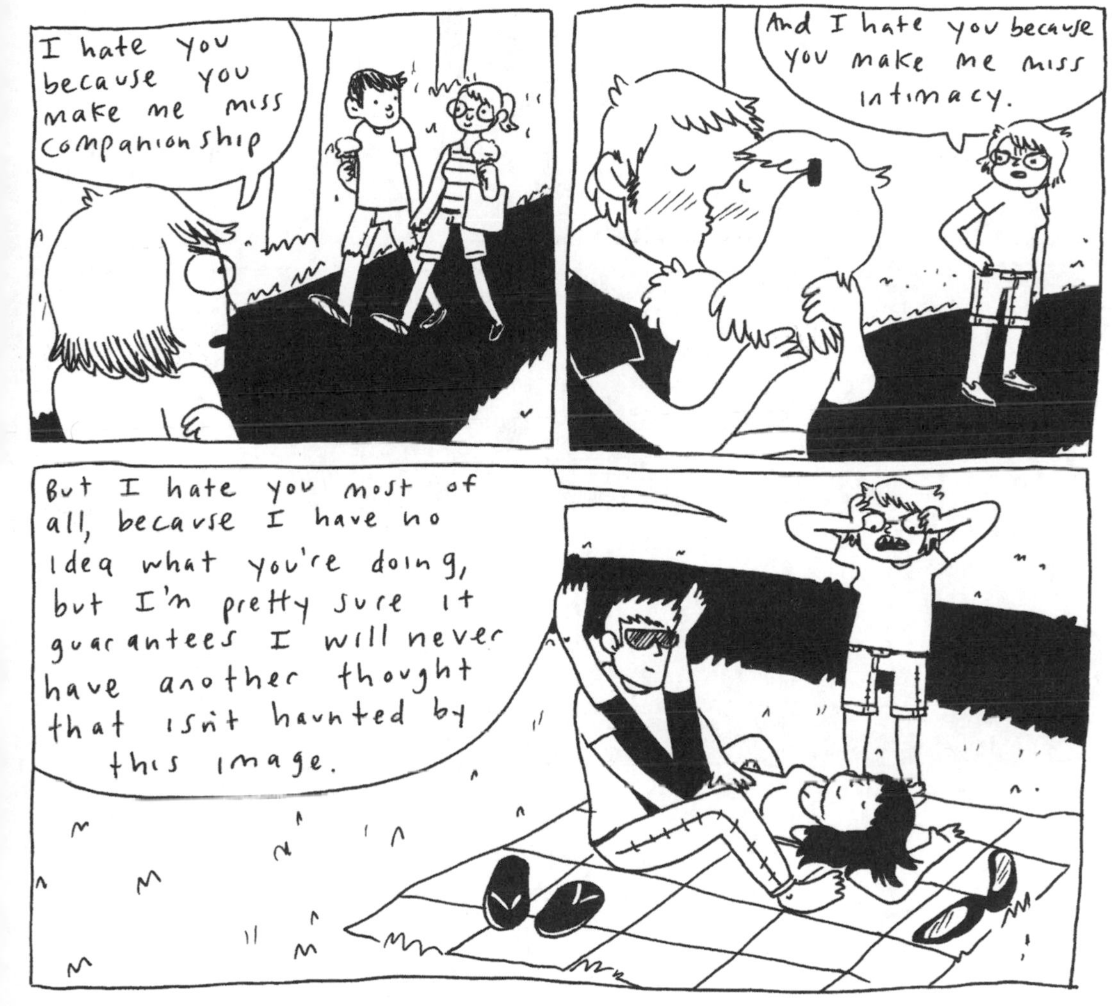
I hate you because you make me miss companionship
And I hate you because you make me miss intimacy.
But I hate you most of all, because I have no idea what you're doing, but I'm pretty sure it guarantees I will never have another thought that isn't haunted by this image.

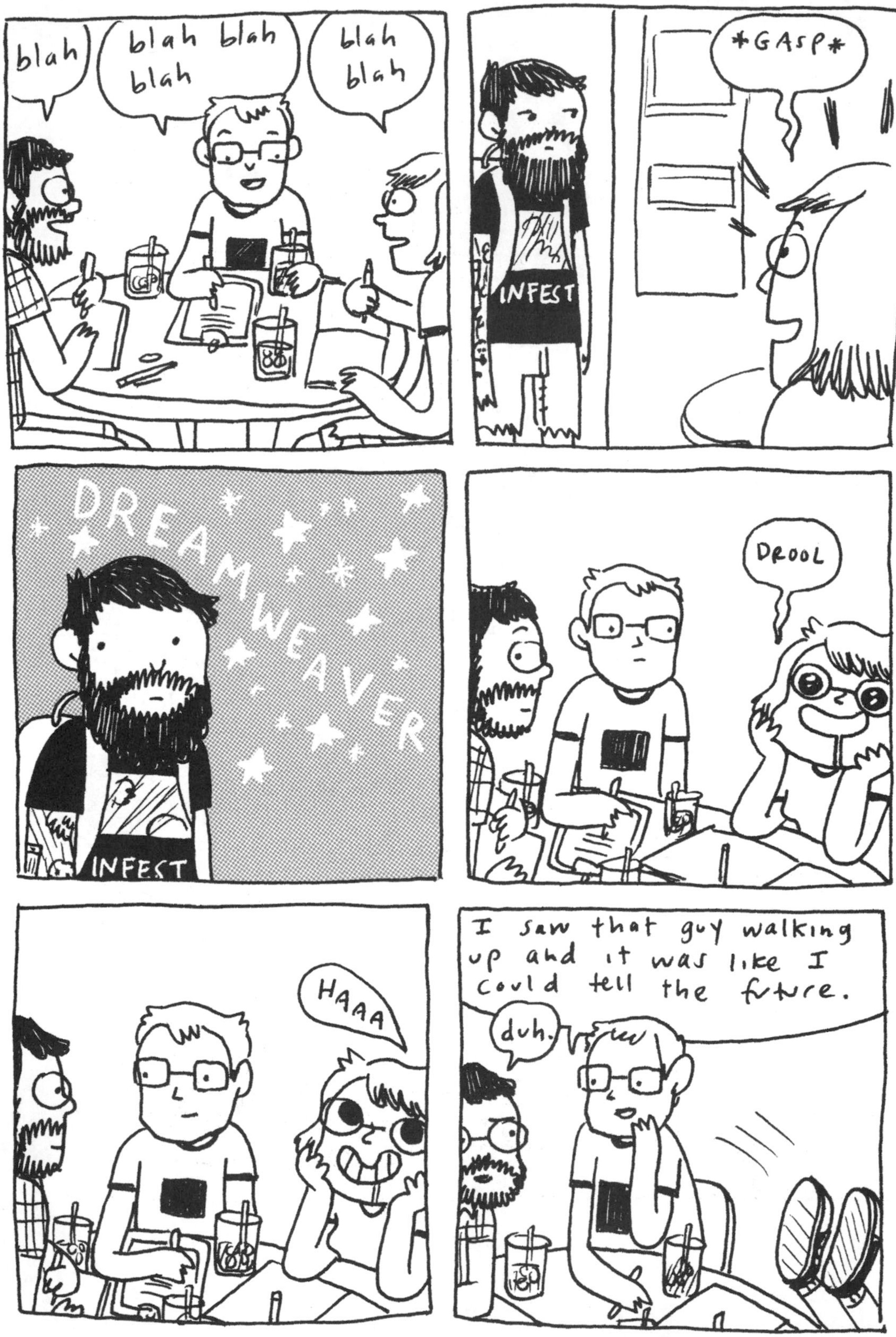
blah
blah blah blah
blah blah
INFEST
GASP
DREAMWEAVER
INFEST
DROOL
HAAA
I saw that guy walking up and it was like I could tell the future.
duh.

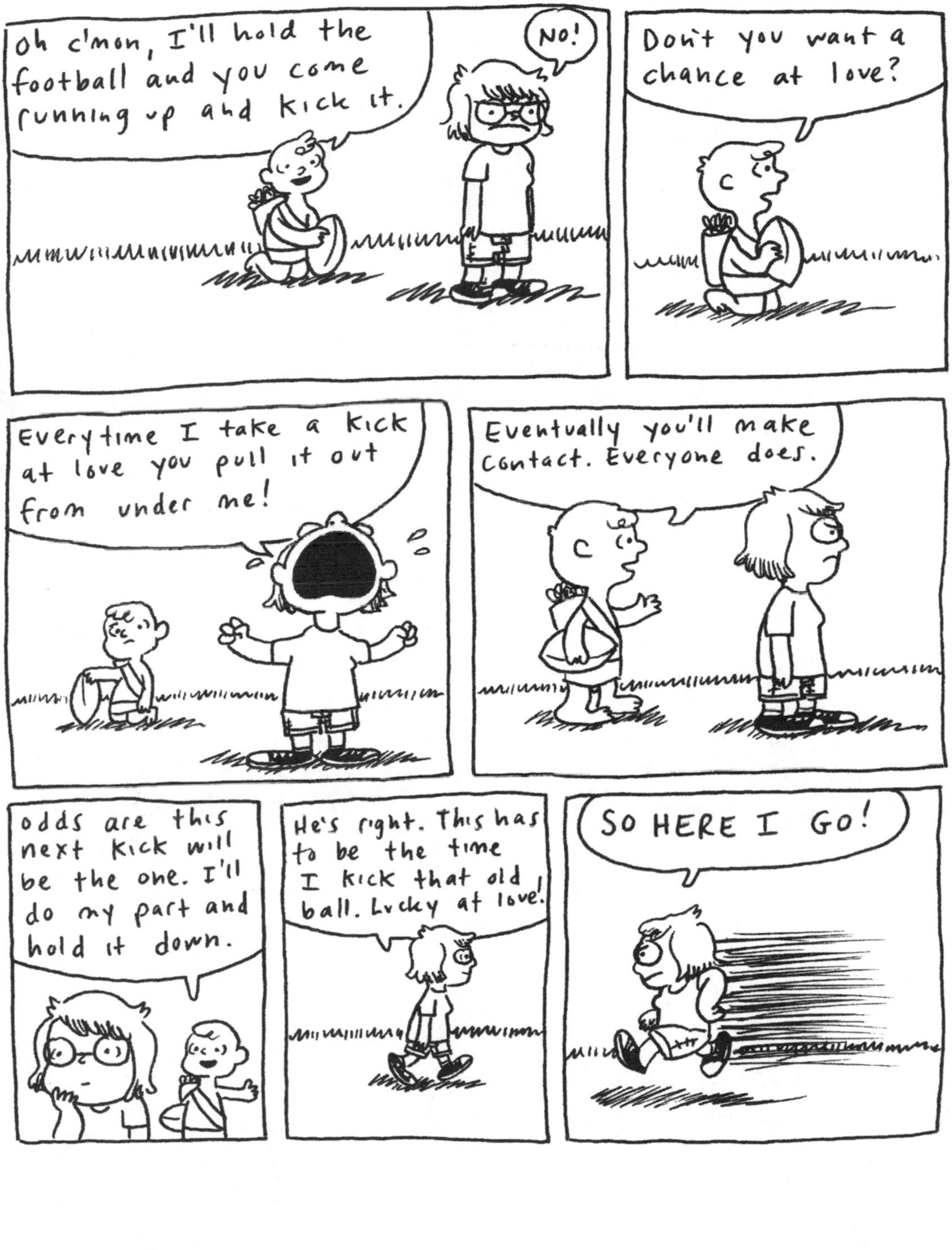
Oh c'mon, I'll hold the football and you come running up and kick it.
No!
Don't you want a chance at love?
Everytime I take a kick at love you pull it out from under me!
Eventually you'll make contact. Everyone does.
Odds are this next kick will be the one. I'll do my part and hold it down.
He's right. This has to be the time I kick that old ball. Lucky at love!
SO HERE I GO!

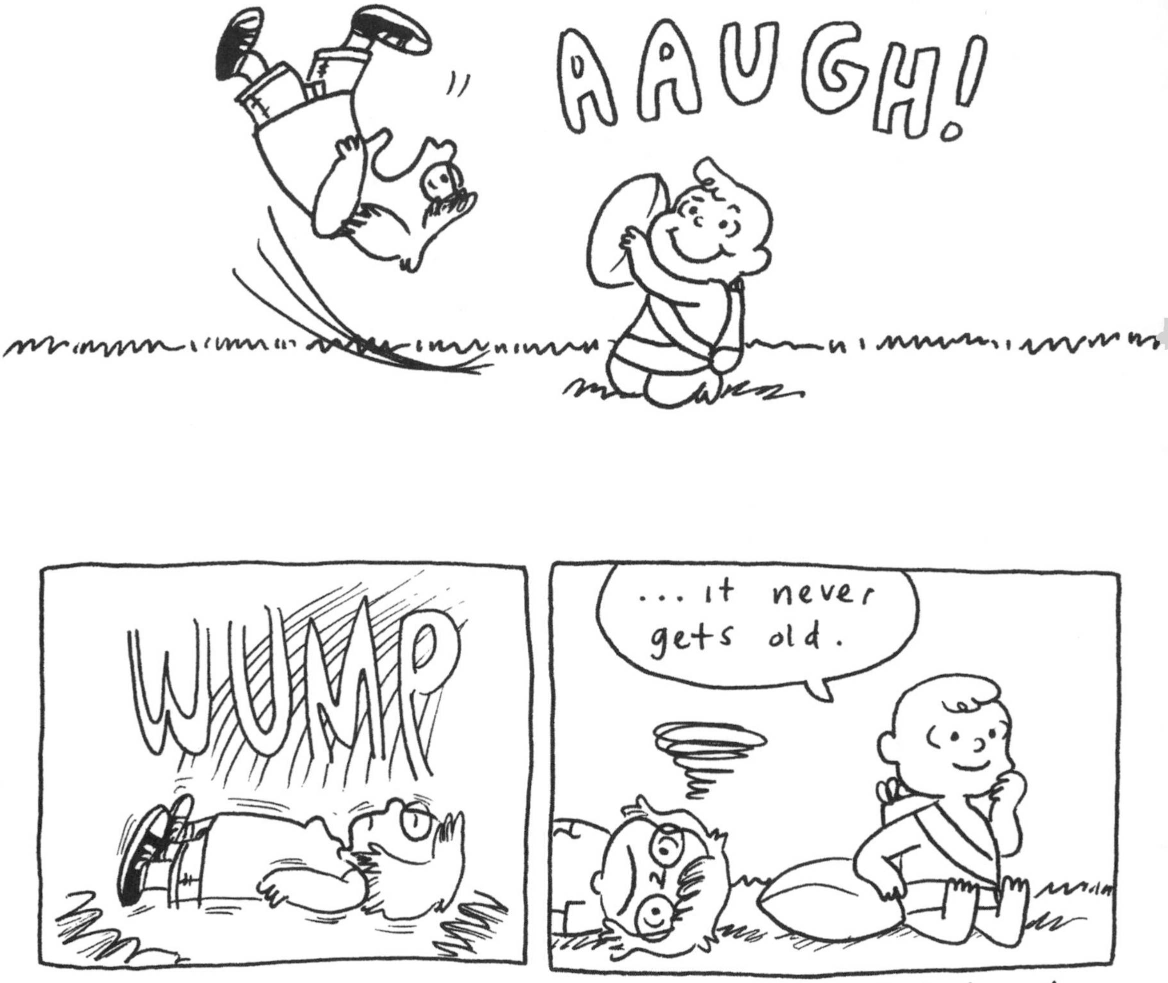
AAUGH!
WUMP
... it never gets old.
GOOD GRIEF!

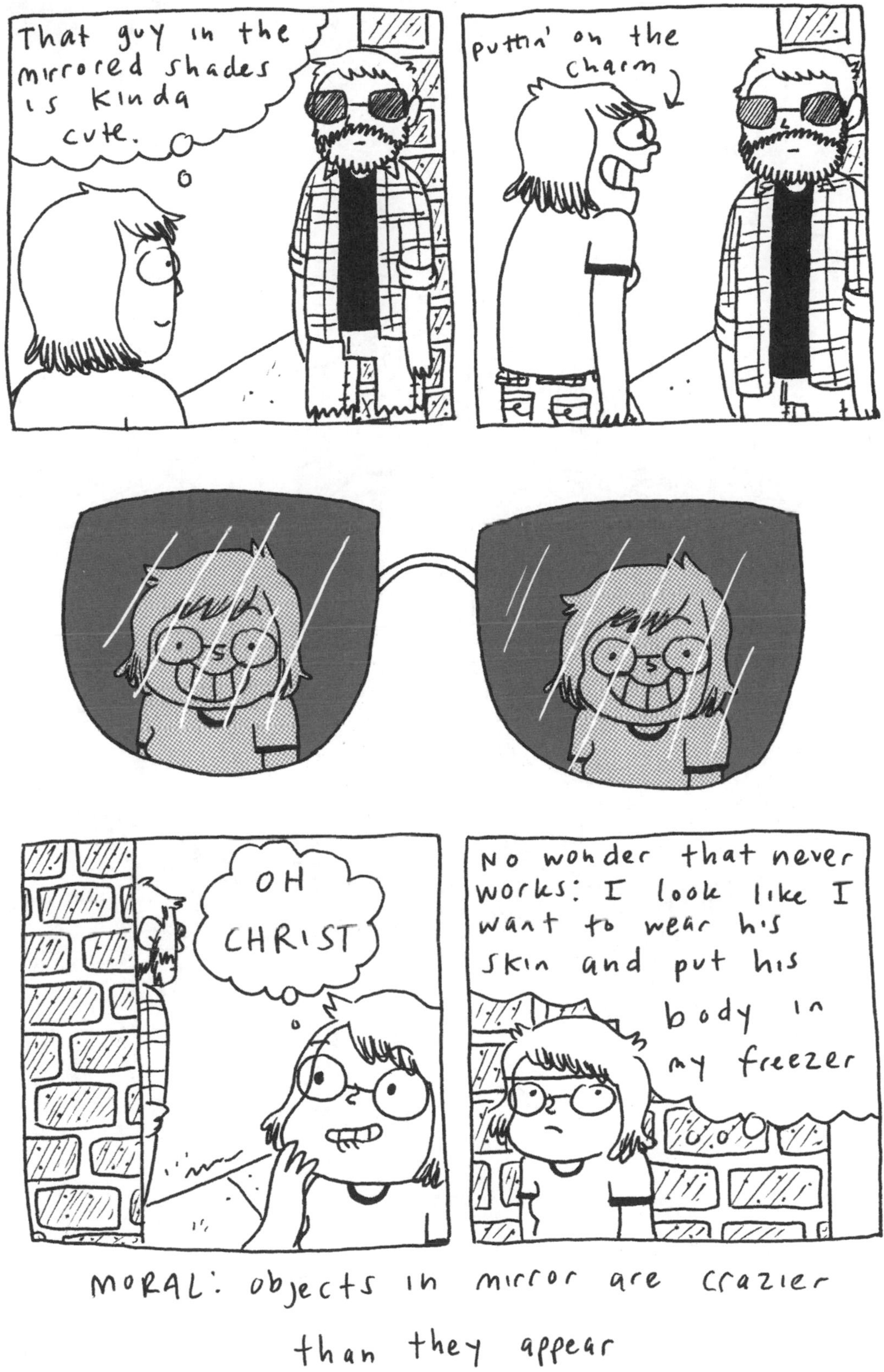
That guy in the mirrored shades is kinda cute.
puttin' on the charm
OH CHRIST
No wonder that never works: I look like I want to wear his skin and put his body in my freezer

MORAL: objects in mirror are crazier than they appear

The one where Liz gets hit on in a bookstore

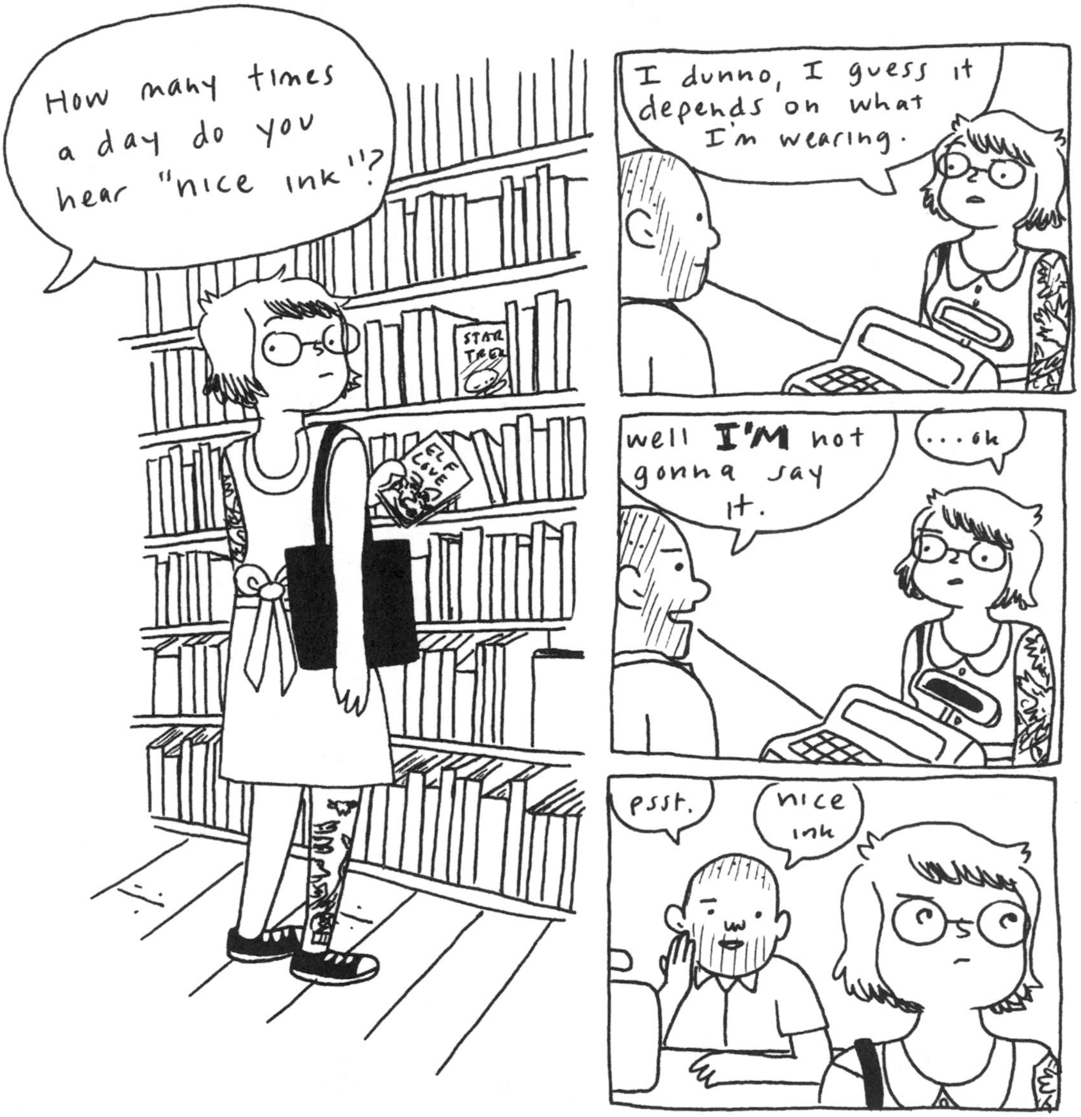
How many times a day do you hear "nice ink"?
STAR TREK
ELF LOVE
I dunno, I guess it depends on what I'm wearing.
well I'M not gonna say it.
...ok
psst.
nice ink

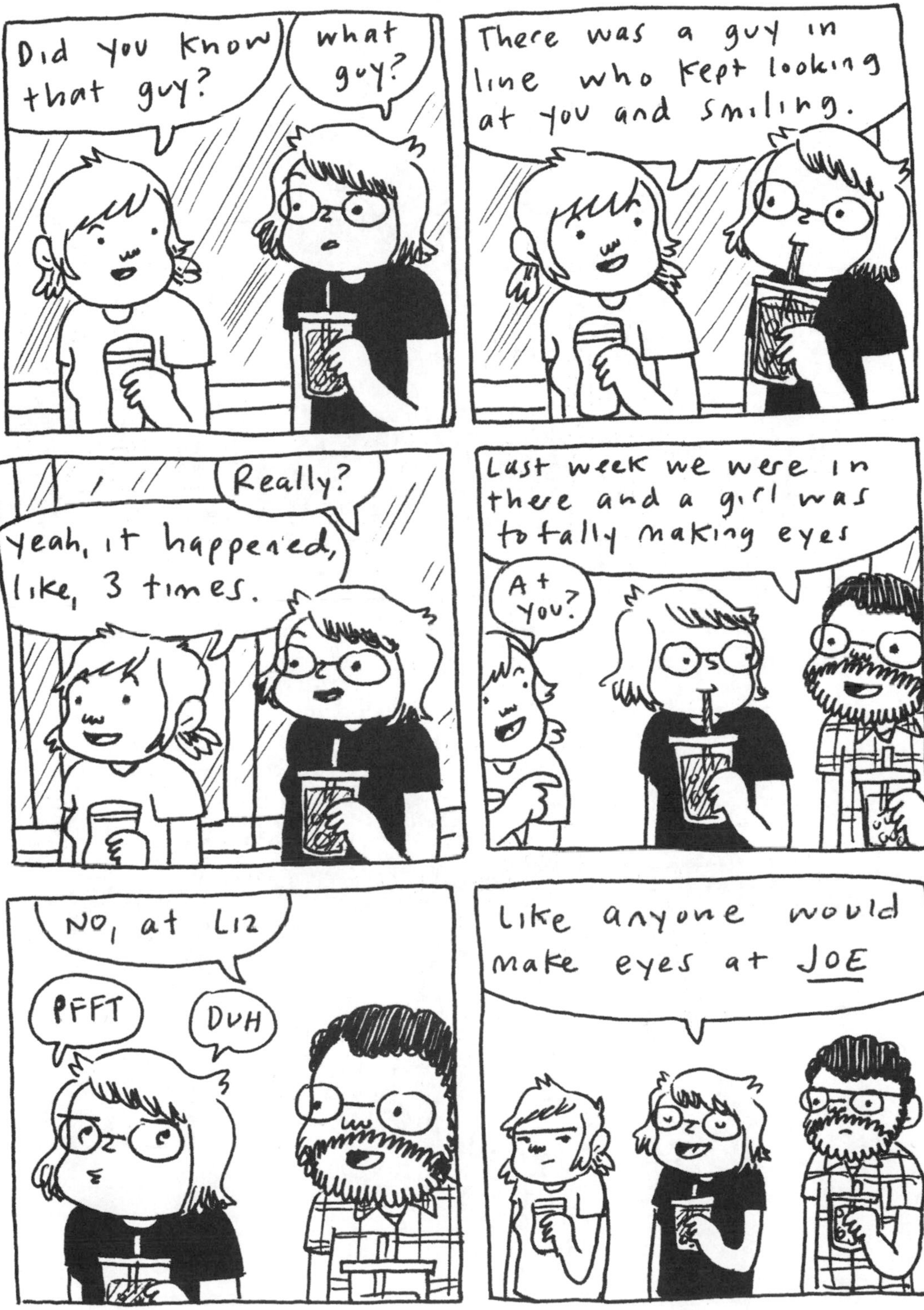
Did you know that guy?
what guy?
There was a guy in line who kept looking at you and smiling.
Really?
yeah, it happened, like, 3 times.
Last week we were in there and a girl was totally making eyes
At you?
No, at Liz
PFFT
DUH
Like anyone would make eyes at JOE

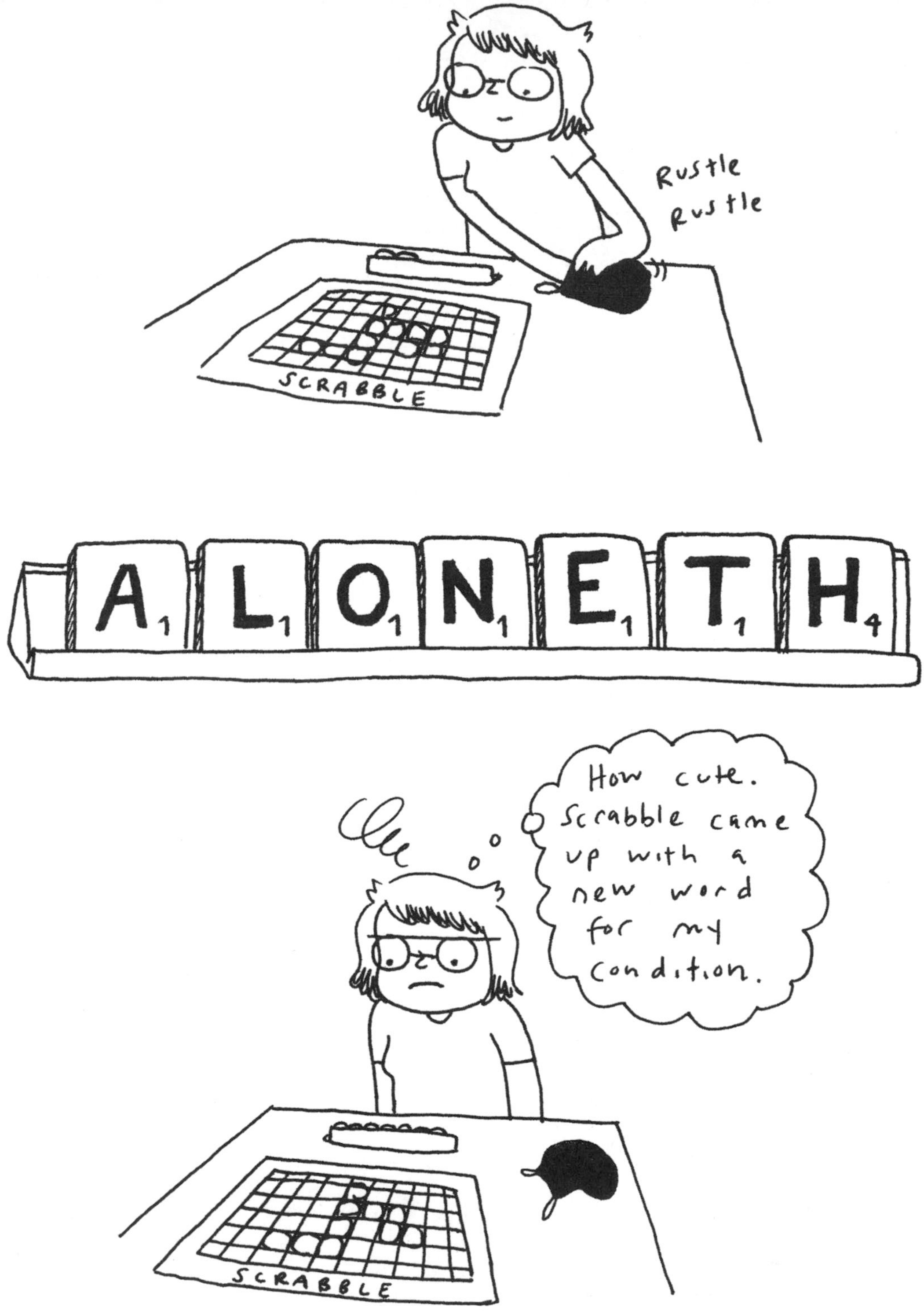
Rustle
Rustle
SCRABBLE
A1 L1 O1 N1 E1 T1 H4
How cute. Scrabble came up with a new word for my condition.
SCRABBLE

...and I couldn't even find a place to play it.

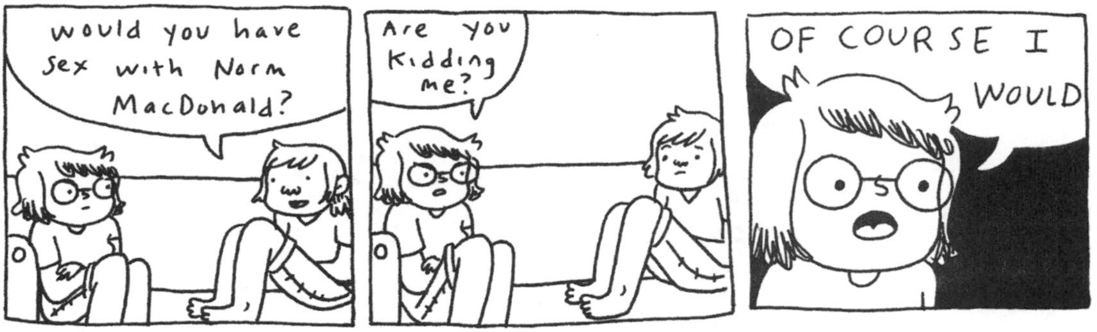
would you have sex with Norm MacDonald?
Are you kidding me?
OF COURSE I WOULD

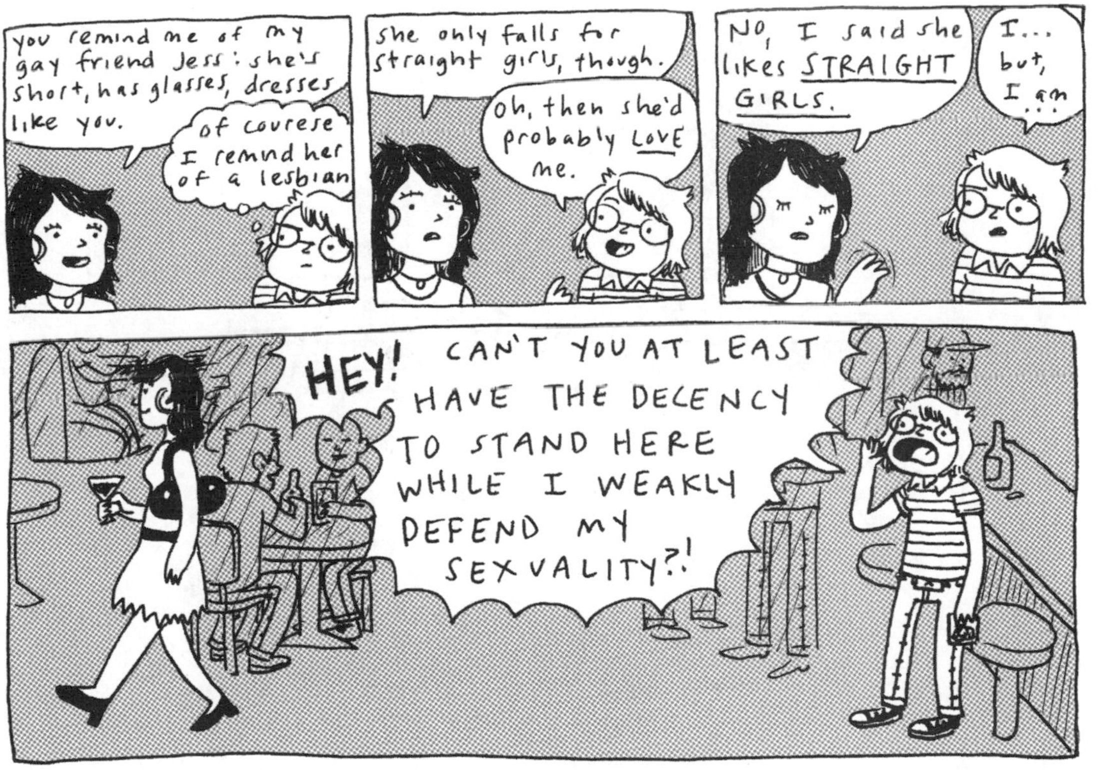
you remind me of my gay friend Jess: she's short, has glasses, dresses like you.
of courese I remind her of a lesbian
she only falls for straight girls, though.
Oh, then she'd probably LOVE me.
No, I said she likes STRAIGHT GIRLS.
I... but, I am...
HEY! CAN'T YOU AT LEAST HAVE THE DECENCY TO STAND HERE WHILE I WEAKLY DEFEND MY SEXUALITY?!

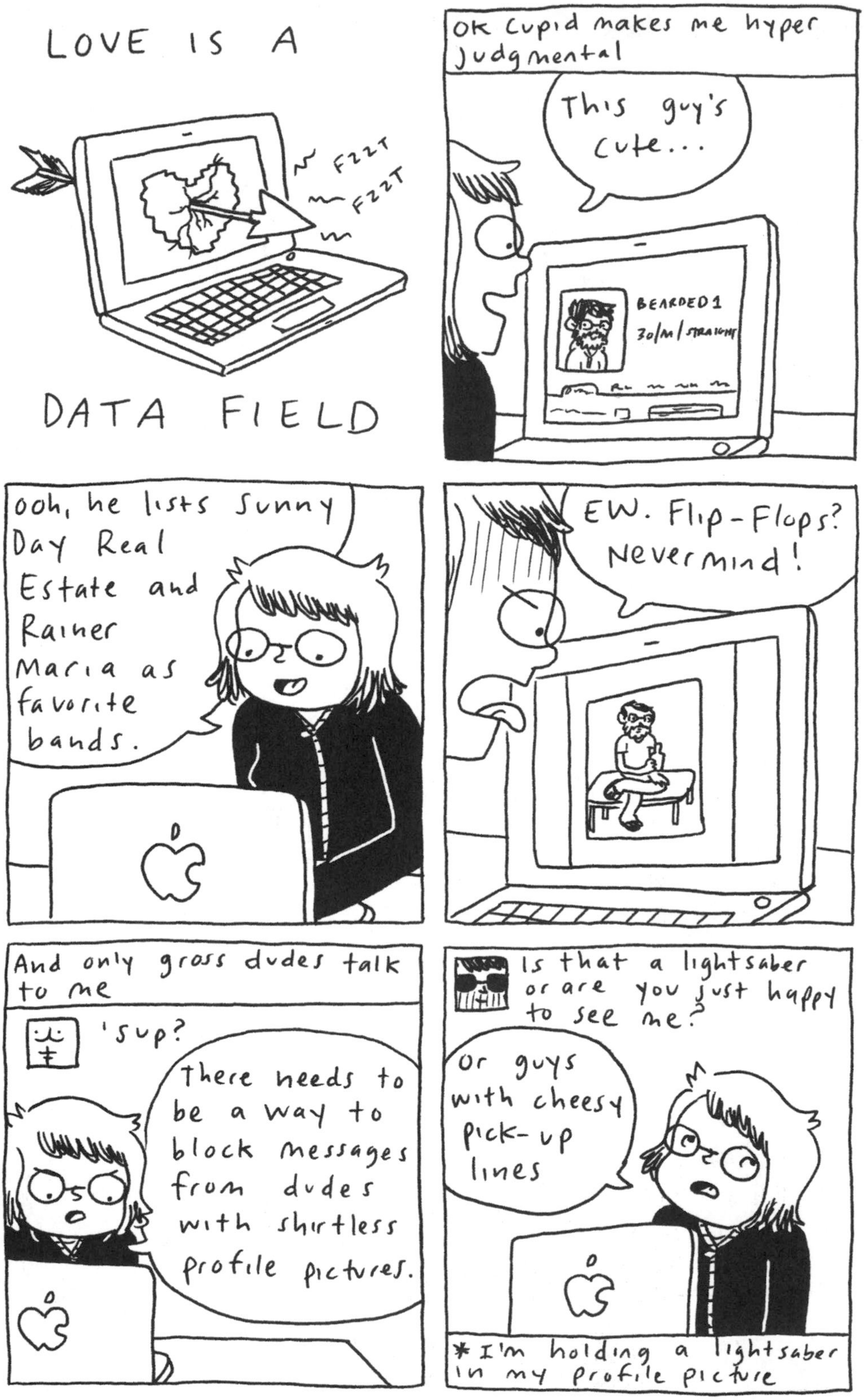
LOVE IS A DATA FIELD
FZZT
FZZT
OK Cupid makes me hyper judgmental
This guy's cute...
BEARDED1
30/M/STRAIGHT
ooh, he lists Sunny Day Real Estate and Rainer Maria as favorite bands.
EW. Flip-Flops? Nevermind!
And only gross dudes talk to me
'sup?
There needs to be a way to block messages from dudes with shirtless profile pictures.
Is that a lightsaber or are you just happy to see me?
Or guys with cheesy pick-up lines
* I'm holding a lightsaber in my profile picture

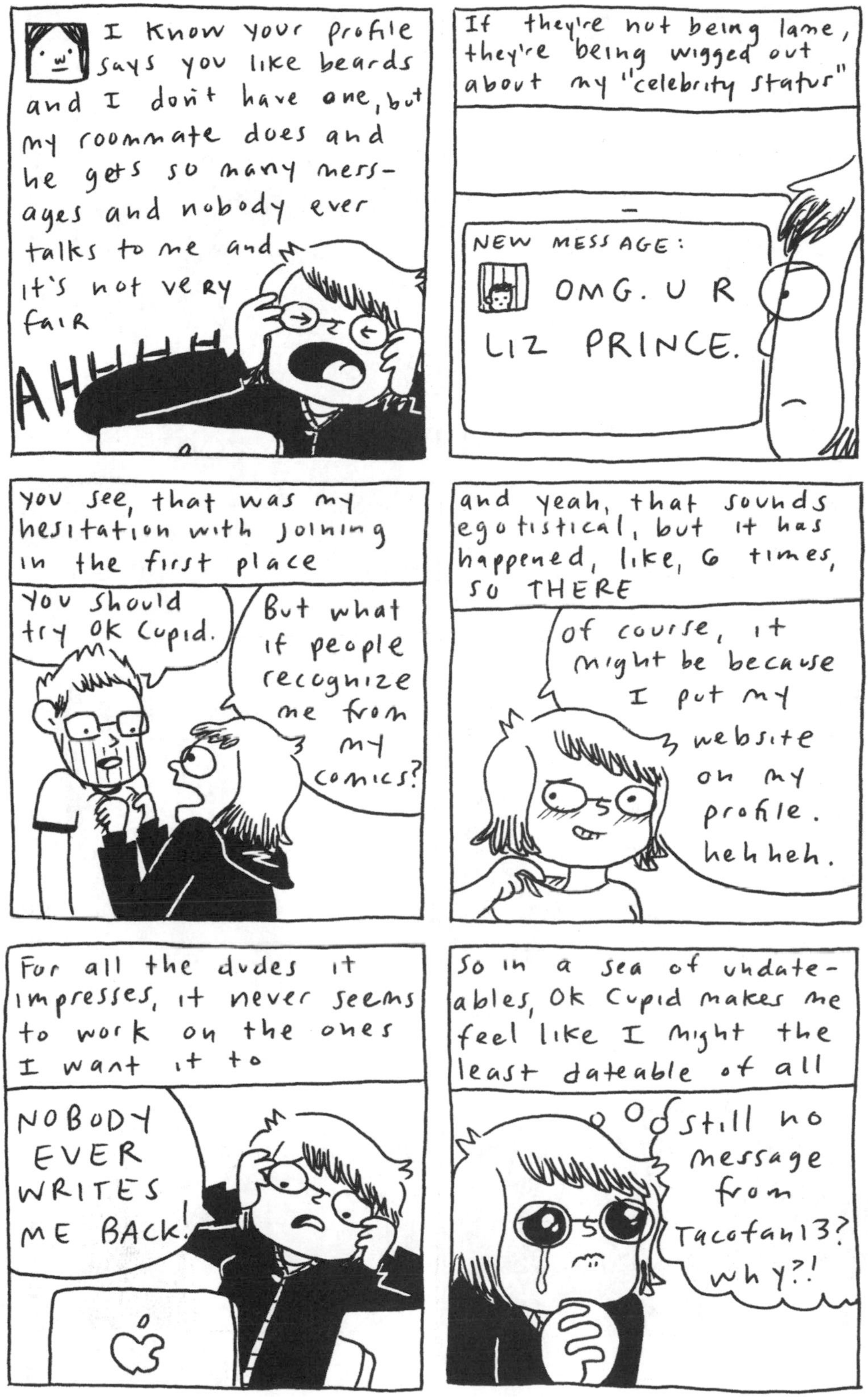
I know your profile says you like beards and I don't have one, but my roommate does and he gets so many messages and nobody ever talks to me and it's not very fair
AHHHH
If they're not being lame, they're being wigged out about my "celebrity status"
NEW MESSAGE:
OMG. U R LIZ PRINCE.
You see, that was my hesitation with joining in the first place
You should try OK Cupid.
But what if people recognize me from my comics?
and yeah, that sounds egotistical, but it has happened, like, 6 times, so THERE
of course, it might be because I put my website on my profile. hehheh.
For all the dudes it impresses, it never seems to work on the ones I want it to
NOBODY EVER WRITES ME BACK!
So in a sea of undateables, Ok Cupid makes me feel like I might the least dateable of all
still no message from Tacofan13? why?!

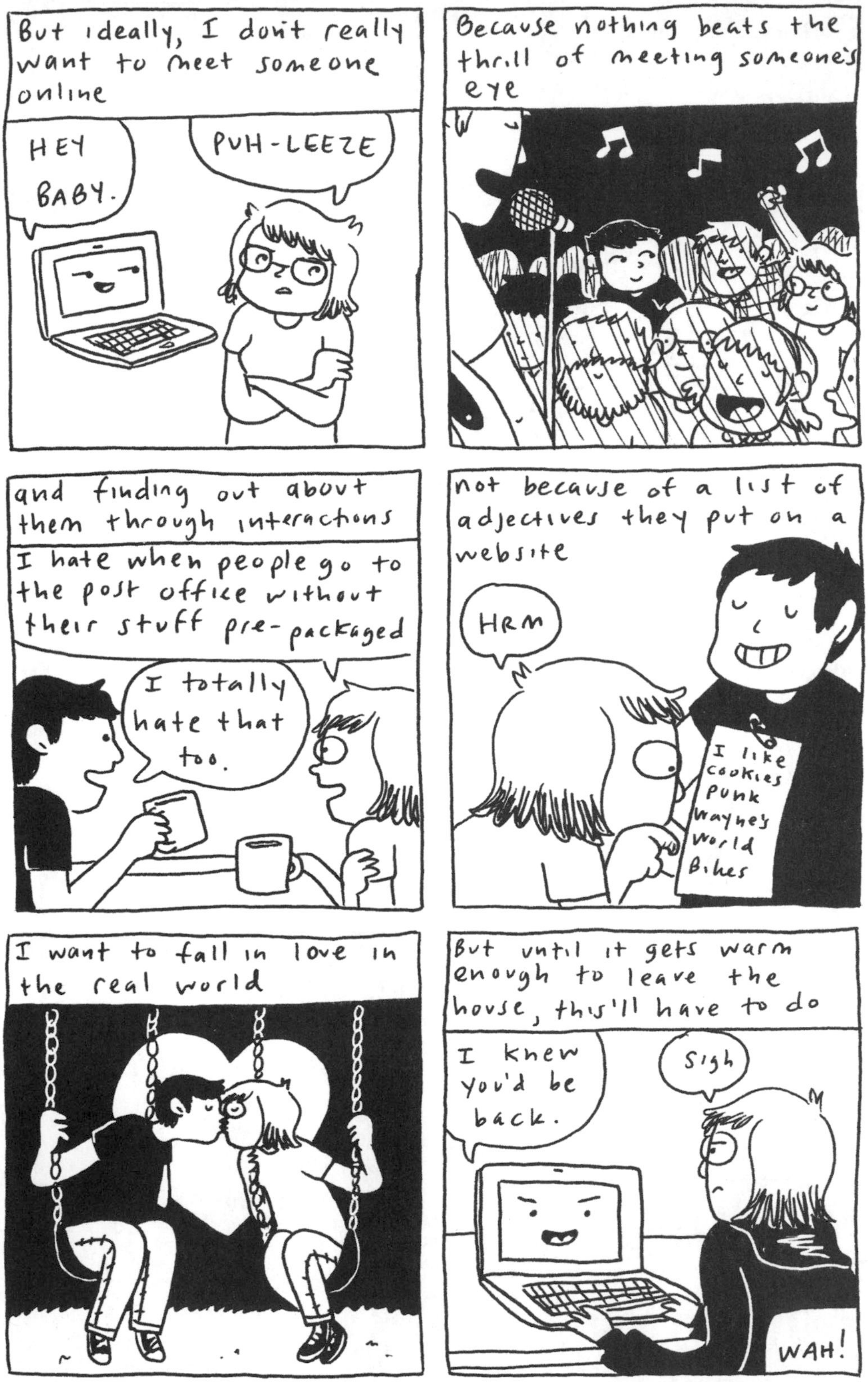
But ideally, I don't really want to meet someone online
HEY BABY.
PUH-LEEZE
Because nothing beats the thrill of meeting someone's eye
and finding out about them through interactions
I hate when people go to the post office without their stuff pre-packaged
I totally hate that too.
not because of a list of adjectives they put on a website
HRM
I like cookies Punk Wayne's World Bikes
I want to fall in love in the real world
But until it gets warm enough to leave the house, this'll have to do
I knew you'd be back.
Sigh
WAH!

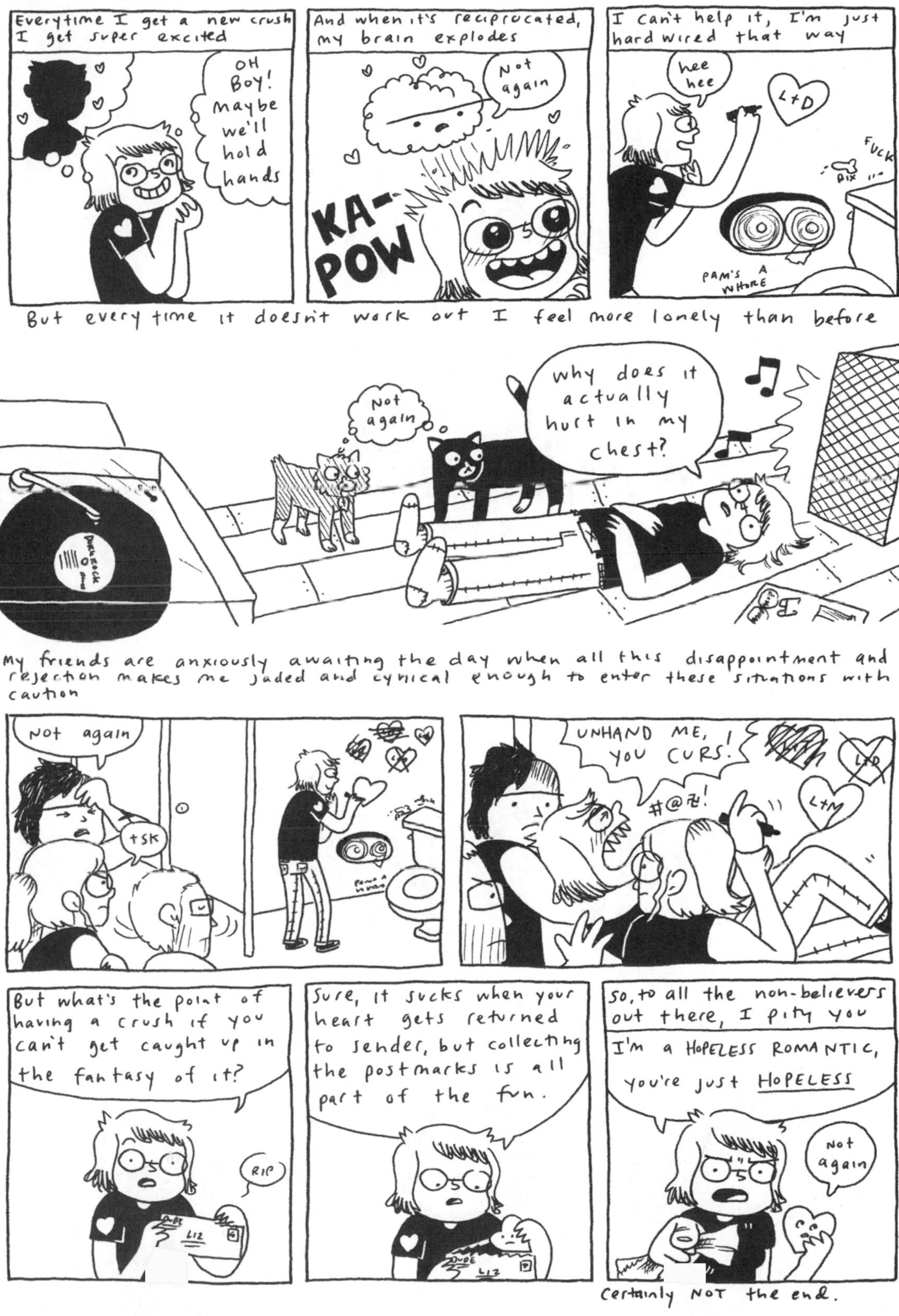
Everytime I get a new crush I get super excited
OH Boy! Maybe we'll hold hands
And when it's reciprocated, my brain explodes
Not again
KA-POW
I can't help it, I'm just hardwired that way
hee hee
L+D
FUCK
PAM'S A WHORE
But every time it doesn't work out I feel more lonely than before
Not again
why does it actually hurt in my chest?
My friends are anxiously awaiting the day when all this disappointment and rejection makes me jaded and cynical enough to enter these situations with caution
Not again
TSK
UNHAND ME, YOU CURS!
#@?!
L+D
L+M
But what's the point of having a crush if you can't get caught up in the fantasy of it?
RIP
DUDE
LIZ
Sure, it sucks when your heart gets returned to sender, but collecting the postmarks is all part of the fun.
DUDE
LIZ
So, to all the non-believers out there, I pity you
I'm a HOPELESS ROMANTIC, you're just HOPELESS
Not again
Certainly NOT the end.

ECATE

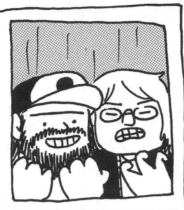

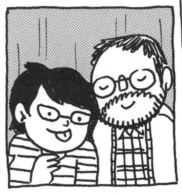

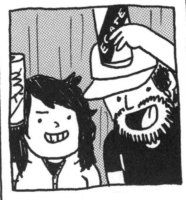

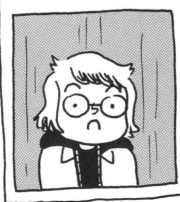

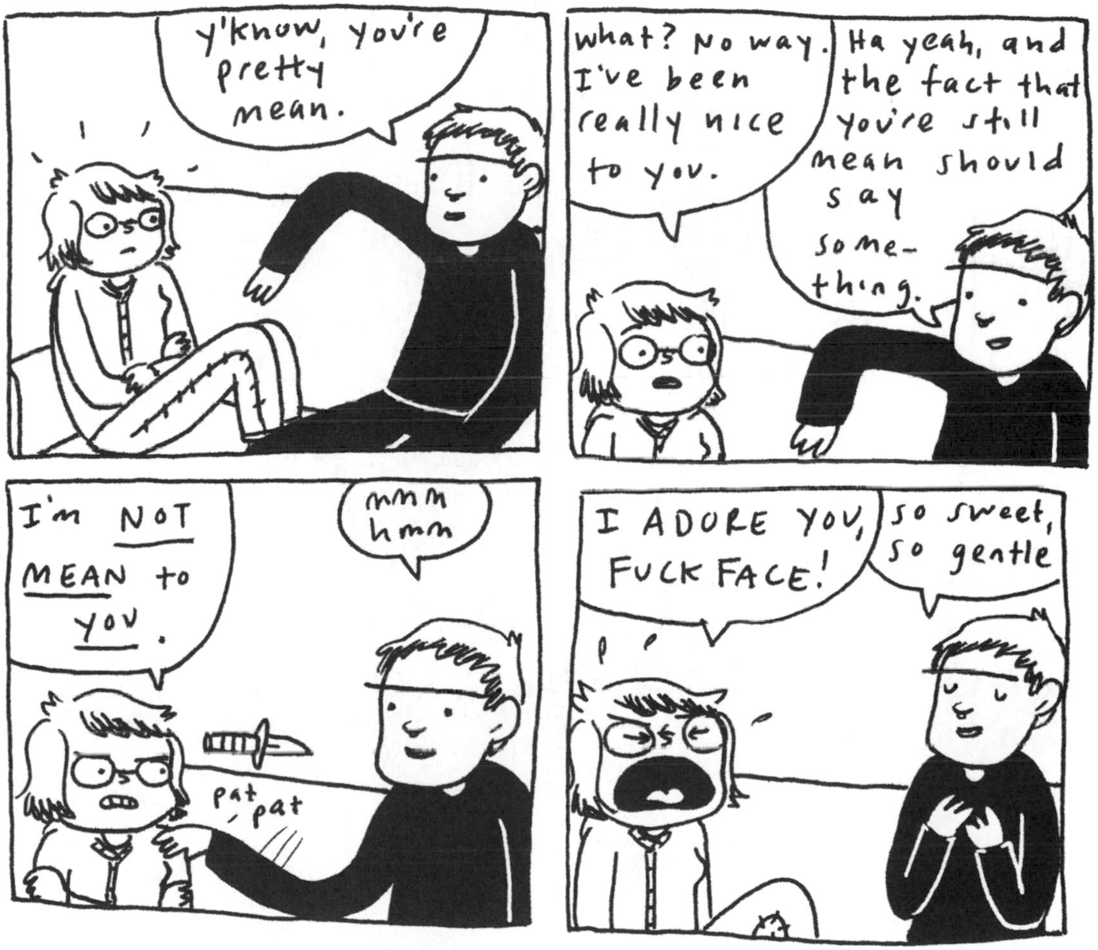
y'know, you're pretty mean.
what? No way. I've been really nice to you.
Ha yeah, and the fact that you're still mean should say some-thing.
I'm NOT MEAN to YOU.
mmm hmm
pat pat
I ADORE YOU, FUCK FACE!
so sweet, so gentle

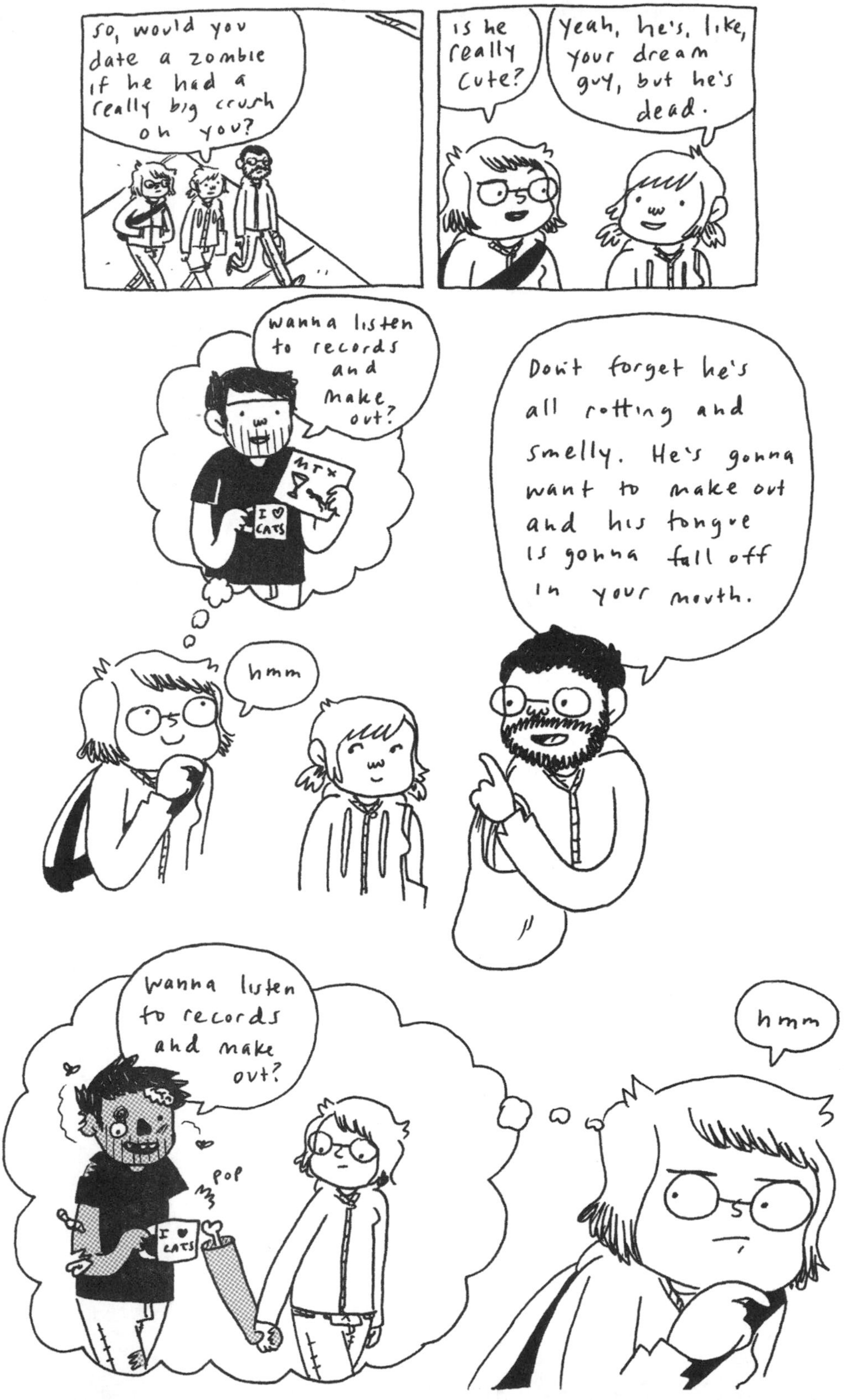
so, would you date a zombie if he had a really big crush on you?
is he really cute?
yeah, he's, like, your dream guy, but he's dead.
wanna listen to records and make out?
MTX
I ♥ CATS
hmm
Don't forget he's all rotting and smelly. He's gonna want to make out and his tongue is gonna fall off in your mouth.
wanna listen to records and make out?
POP
I ♥ CATS
hmm

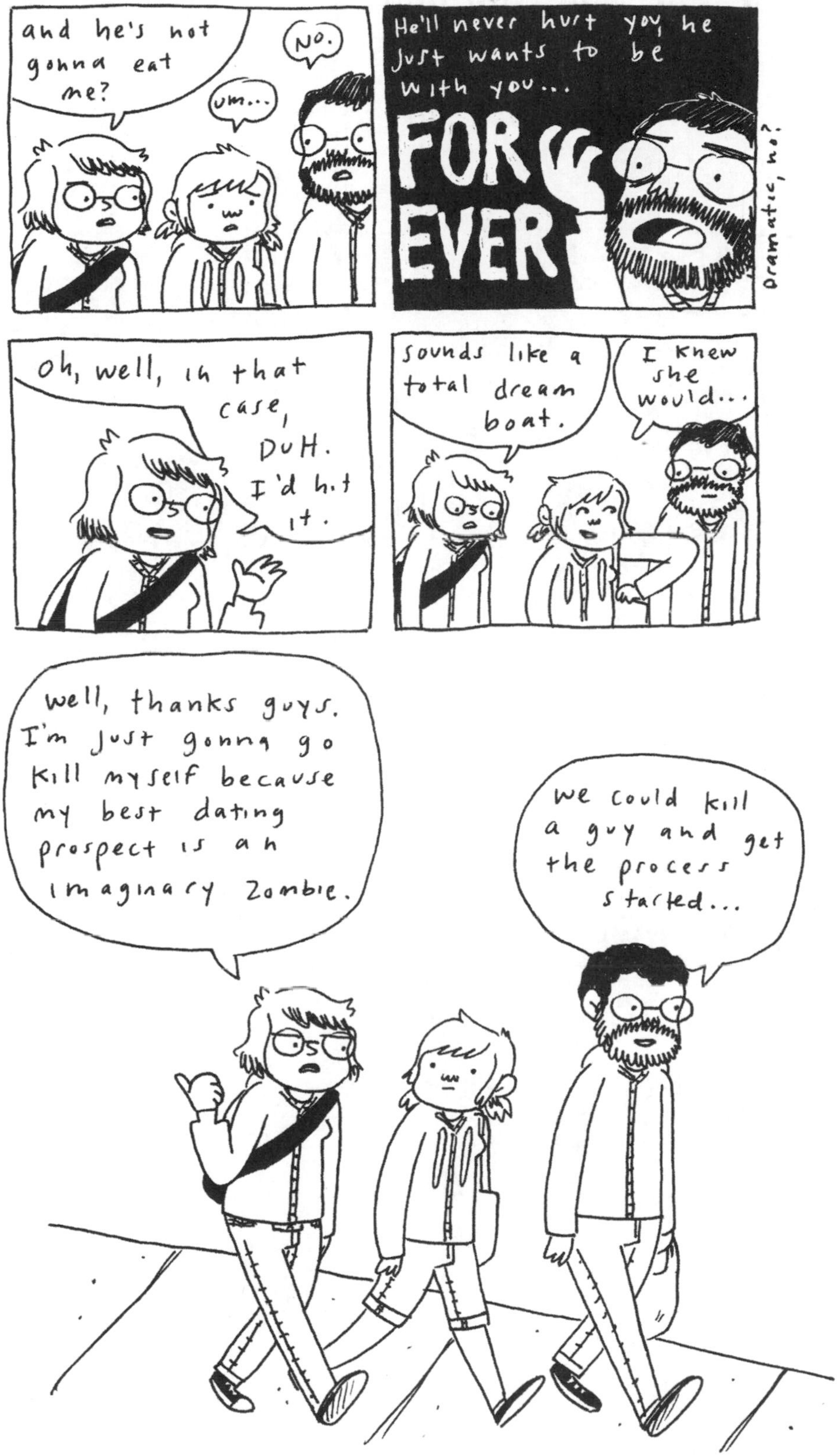
and he's not gonna eat me?
um...
No.
He'll never hurt you, he just wants to be with you...
FOR EVER
Dramatic, no?
Oh, well, in that case, DUH. I'd hit it.
sounds like a total dream boat.
I knew she would...
well, thanks guys. I'm just gonna go kill myself because my best dating prospect is an imaginary zombie.
we could kill a guy and get the process started...

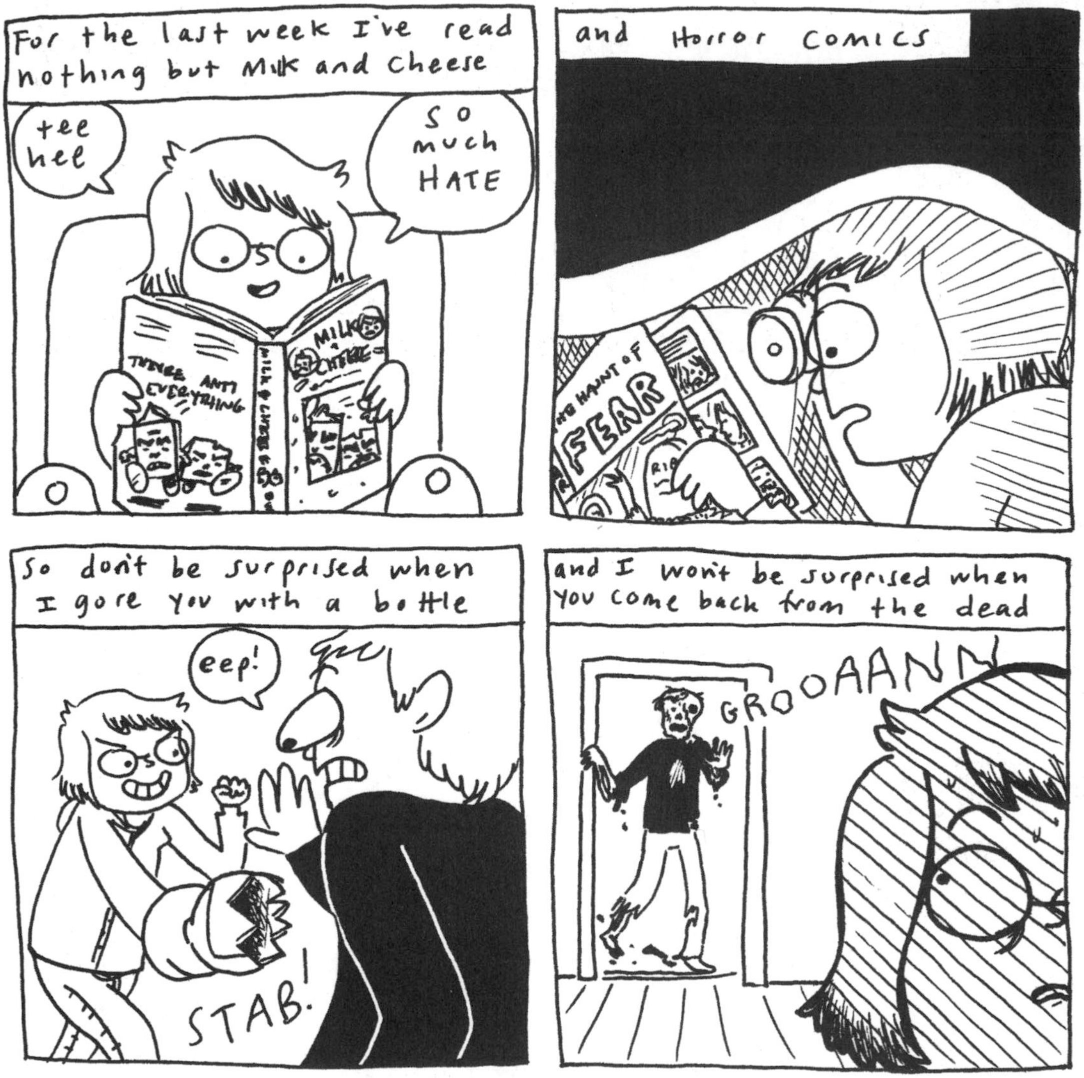
For the last week I've read nothing but Milk and Cheese
tee hee
So much HATE
and Horror comics
FEAR
So don't be surprised when I gore you with a bottle
eep!
STAB!
and I won't be surprised when you come back from the dead
GROOAANN

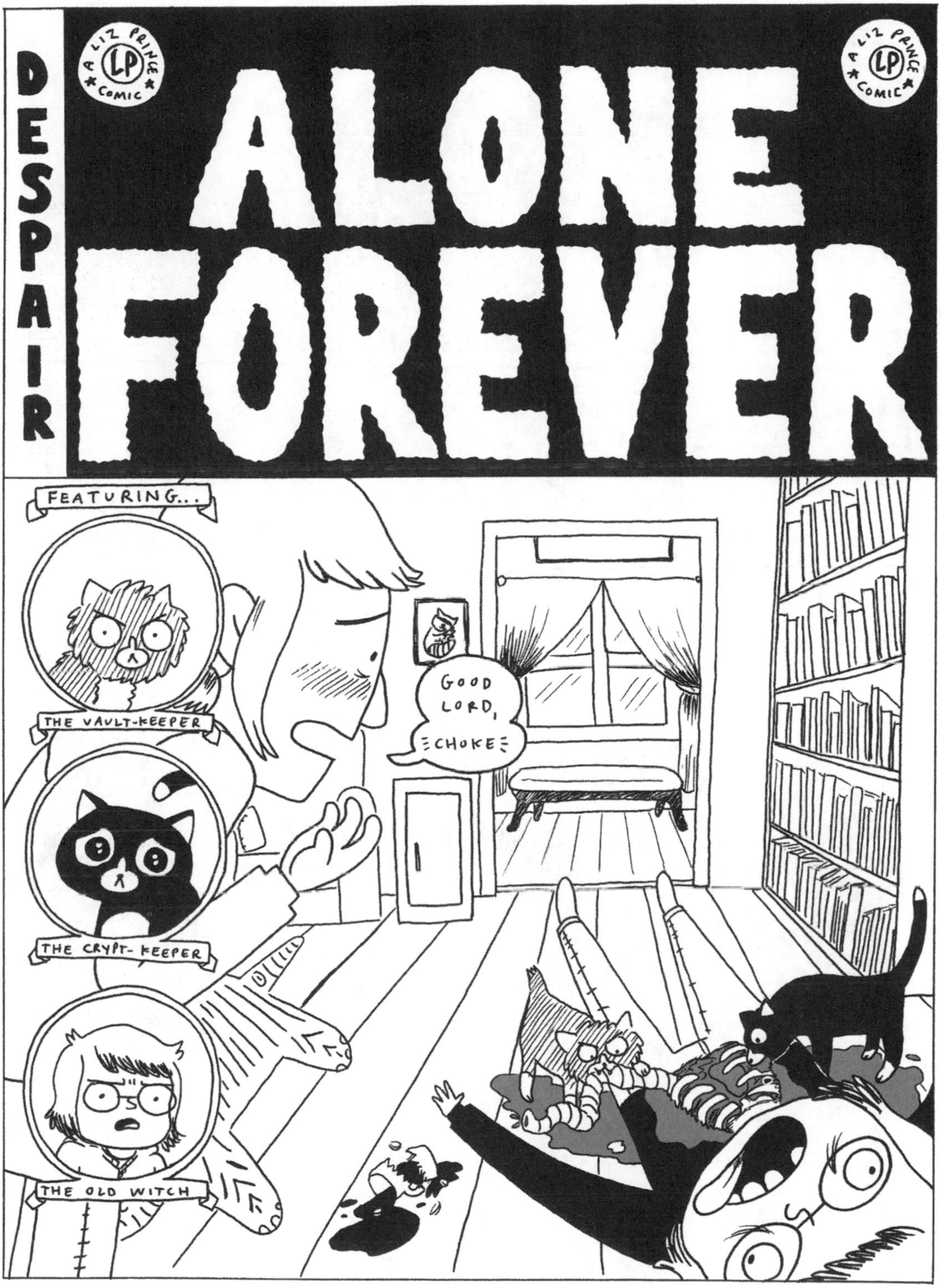
DESPAIR
A LIZ PRINCE COMIC
LP
ALONE FOREVER
A LIZ PRINCE COMIC
LP
FEATURING...
THE VAULT-KEEPER
THE CRYPT-KEEPER
THE OLD WITCH
GOOD LORD,
CHOKE

2012

is so bright, I gotta wear shades

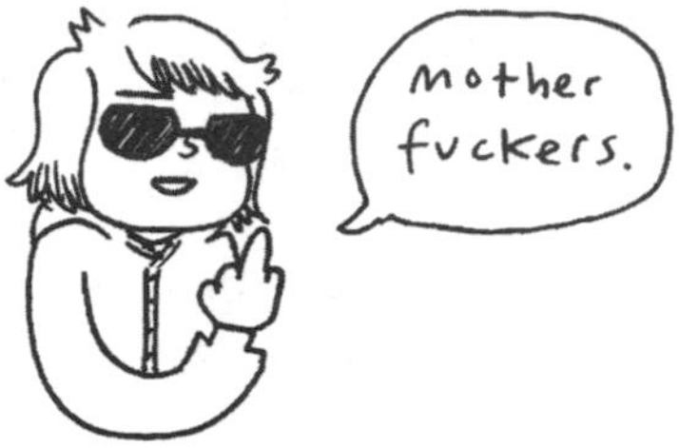
mother fuckers.

I rang in the New Year at a party in Philly, surrounded by some of my favourite people I met in 2011

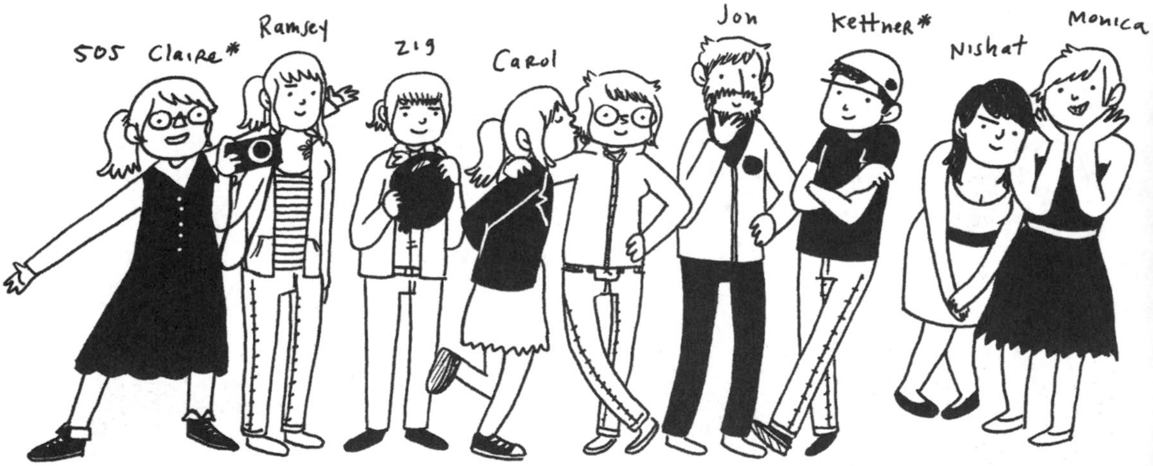
SOS Claire*
Ramsey
Zig
Carol
Jon
Kettner*
Nishat
Monica

* these people I have known FOREVER

and then I spent a night in Brooklyn with my brother, who just moved there a few months ago: it's great to have him back on the east coast

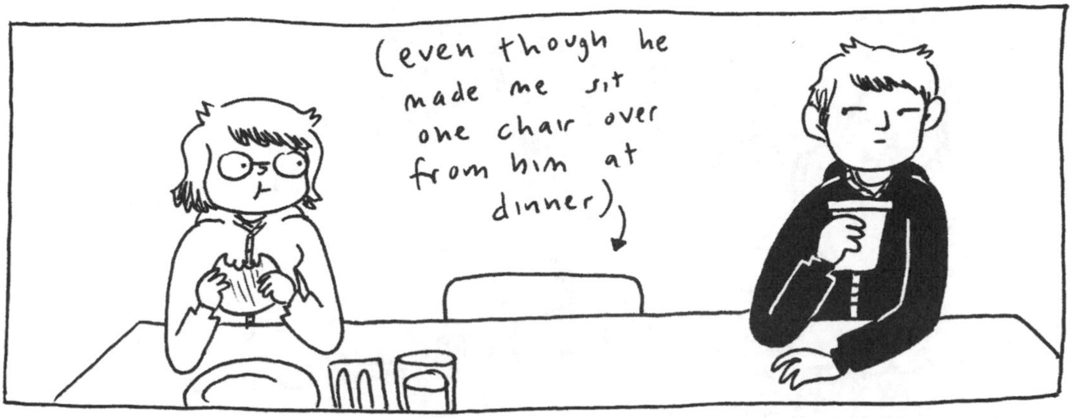
(even though he made me sit one chair over from him at dinner)

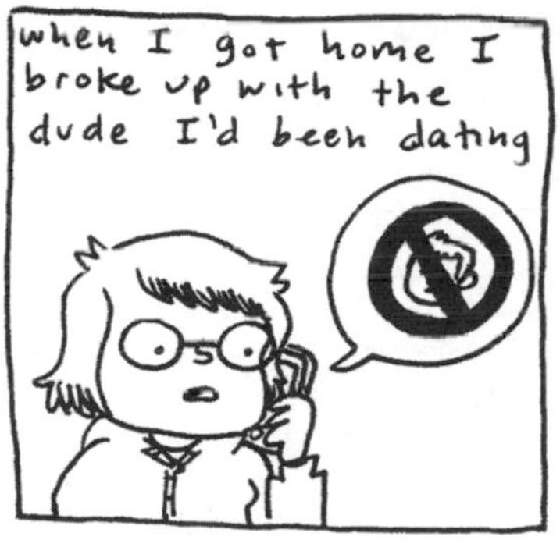
when I got home I broke up with the dude I'd been dating

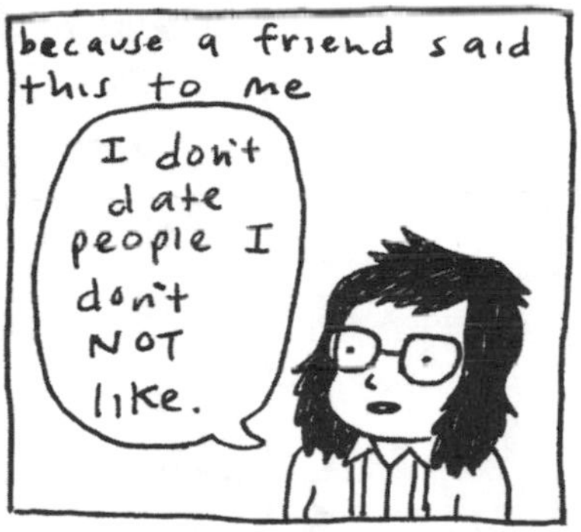
because a friend said this to me
I don't date people I don't NOT like.

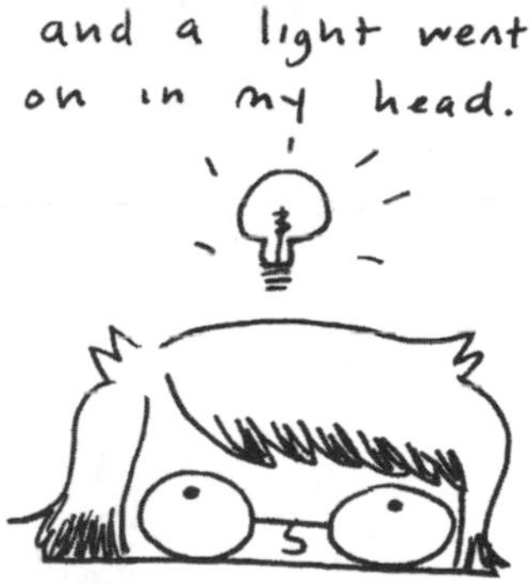
and a light went on in my head.

I have so many friends who totally satisfy my craving for intellectual and emotional fufilment, and although there's nothing physical between us, I'm willing to go without until I meet someone I'm genuinely excited about dating

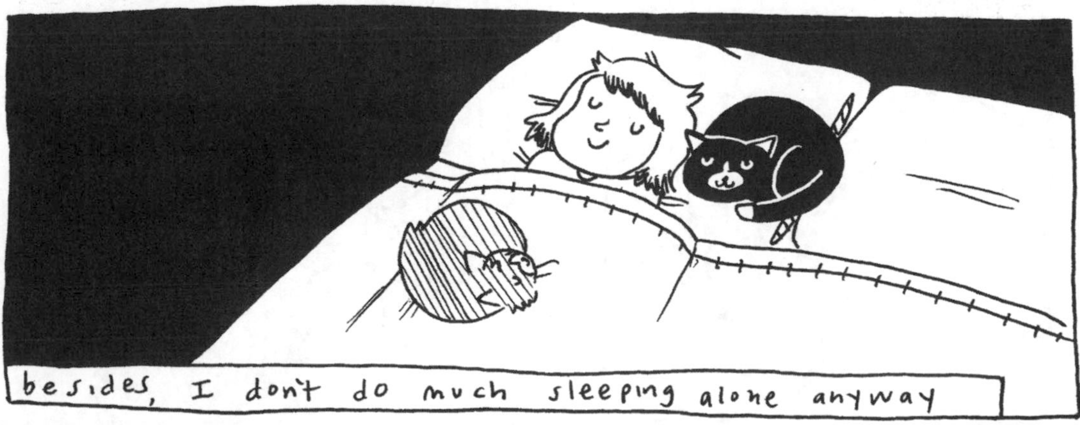
besides, I don't do much sleeping alone anyway

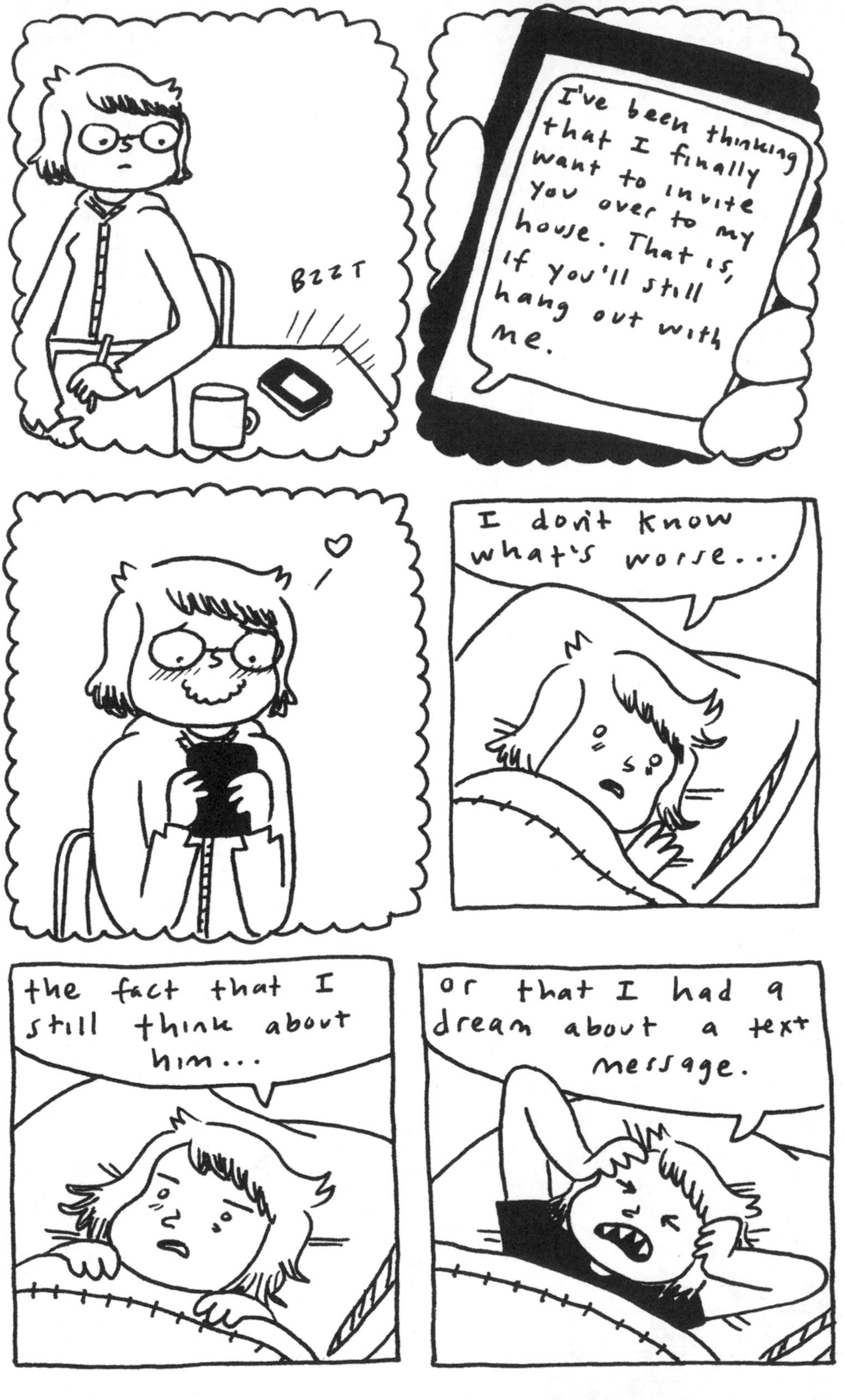
BZZT
I've been thinking that I finally want to invite you over to my house. That is, if you'll still hang out with me.
I don't know what's worse...
the fact that I still think about him...
or that I had a dream about a text message.

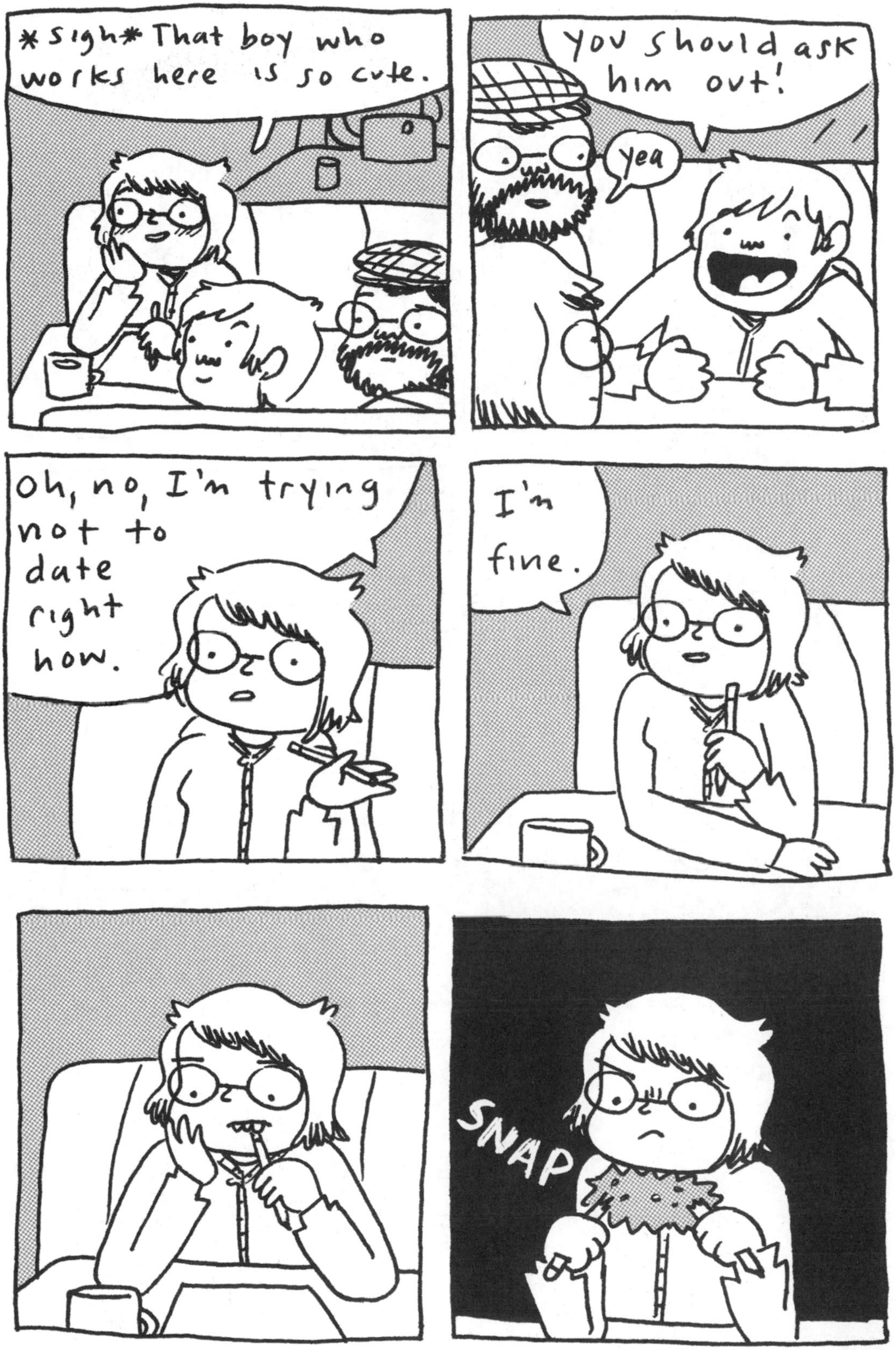
sigh That boy who works here is so cute.
You should ask him out!
yea
Oh, no, I'm trying not to date right now.
I'm fine.
SNAP

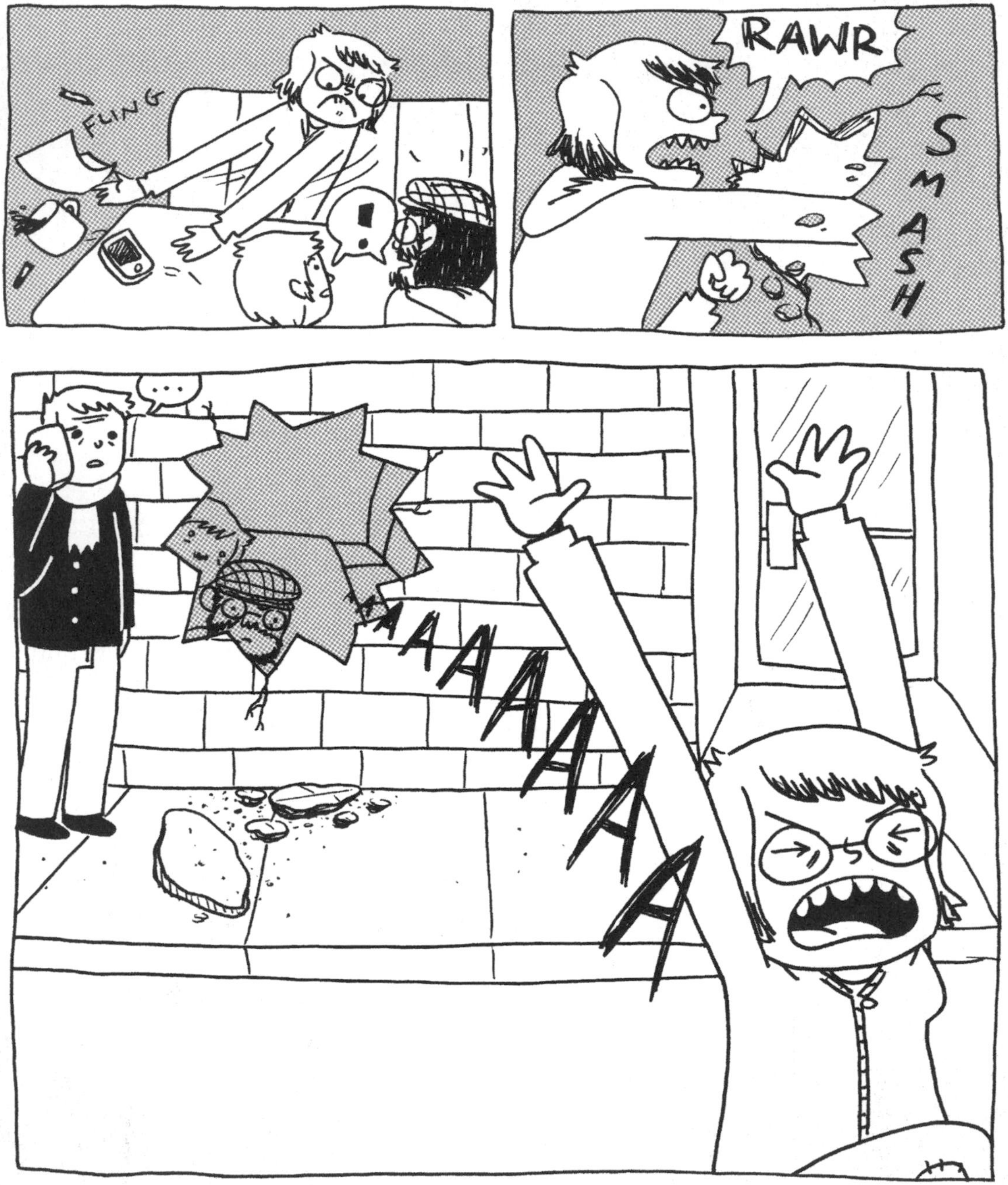
FLING
!
RAWR
SMASH
...
AAAAAAAAAAA

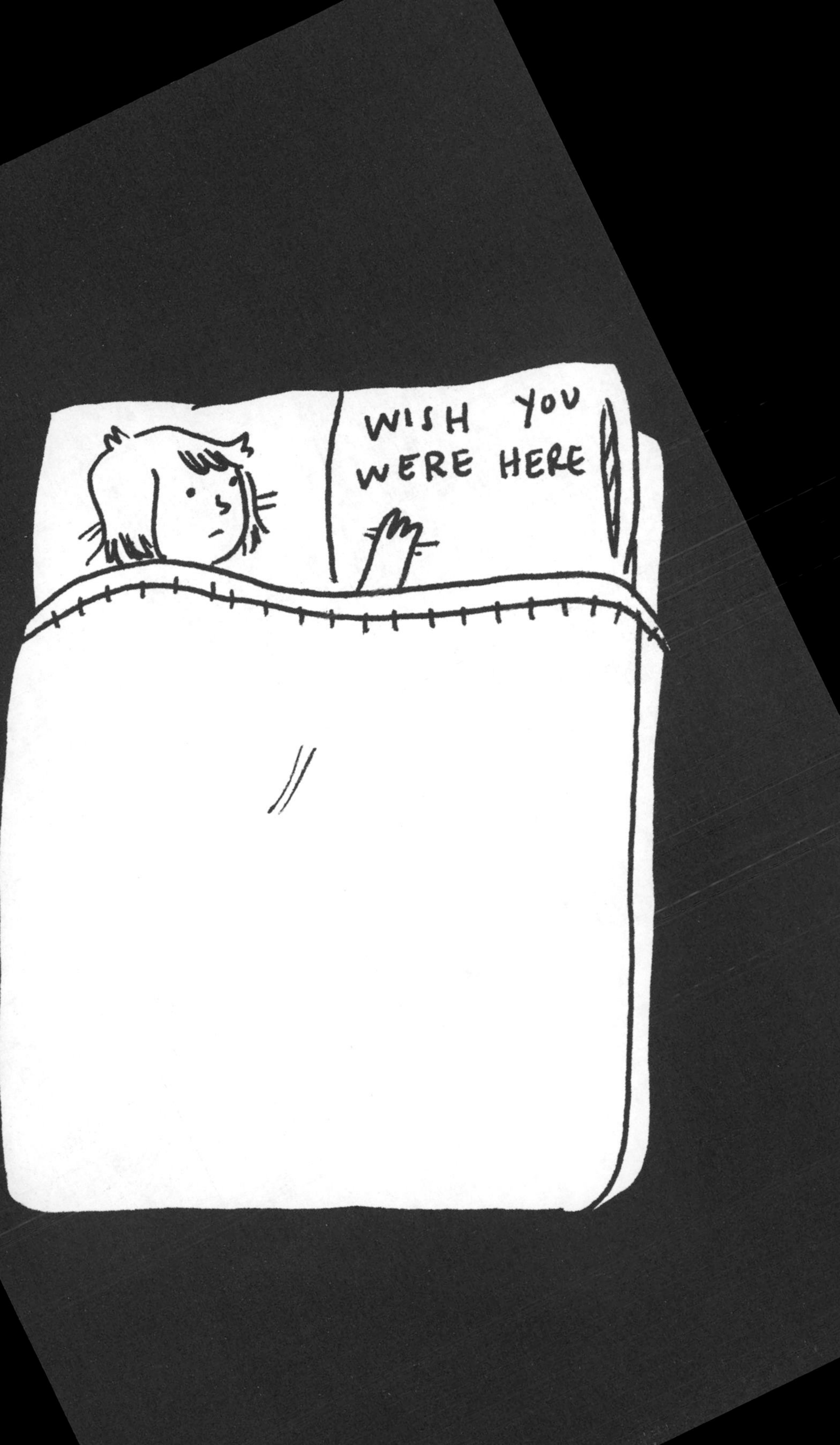
WISH YOU WERE HERE

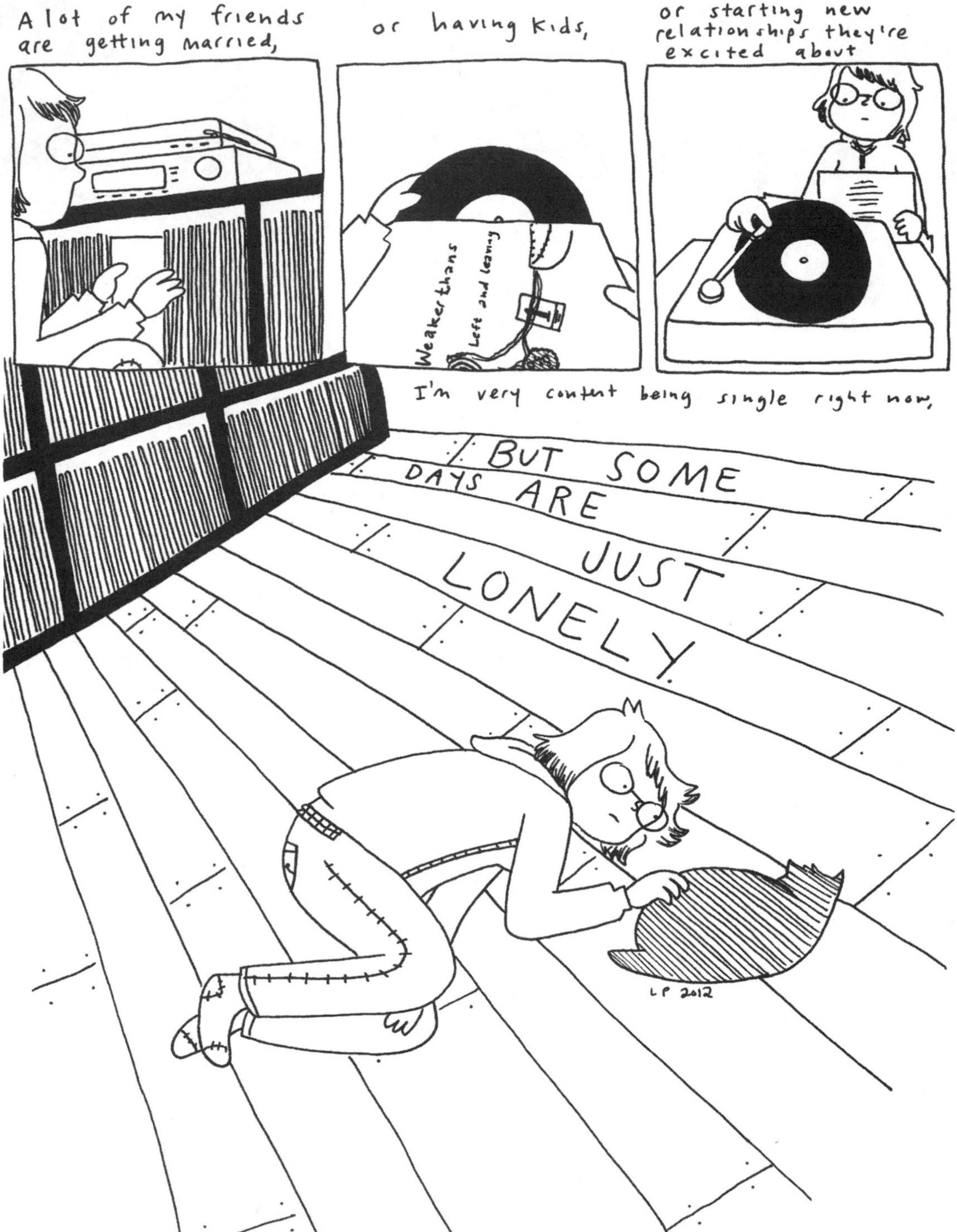
A lot of my friends are getting married,
or having kids,
or starting new relationships they're excited about
Weakerthans
Left and Leaving
I'm very content being single right now,
BUT SOME DAYS ARE JUST LONELY.
LP 2012

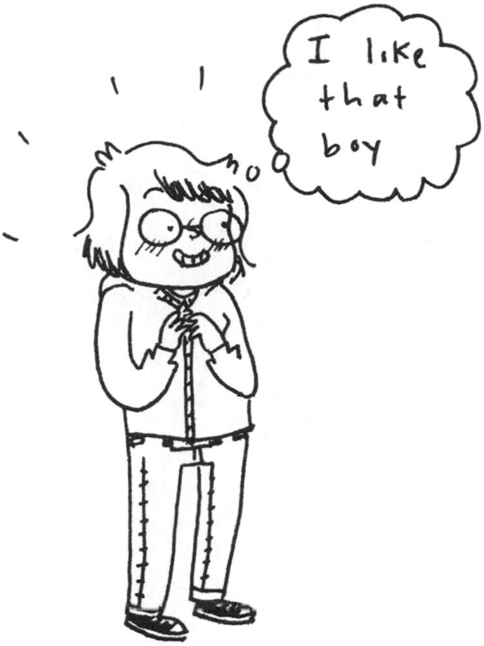
I like that boy

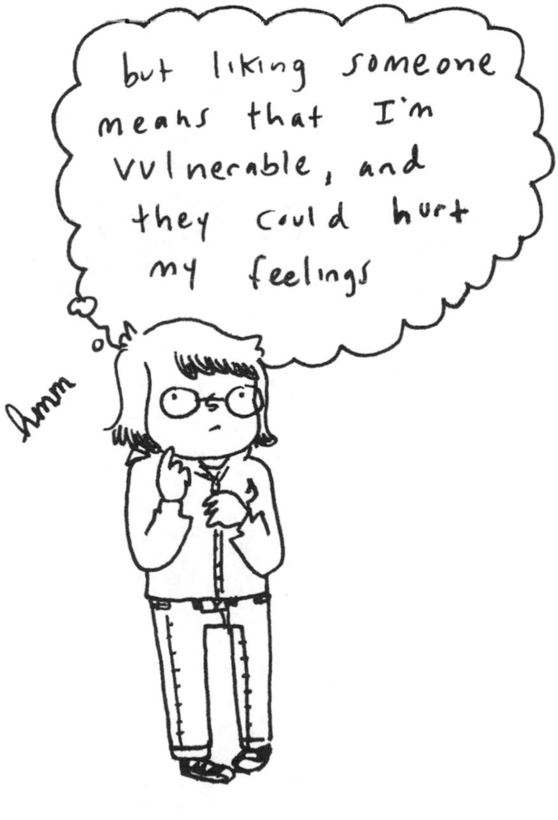
but liking someone means that I'm vulnerable, and they could hurt my feelings
hmm

best pad my insecurities with indifference and sarcasm, that way I won't seem like a wimp
HEY, FUCK YOU!

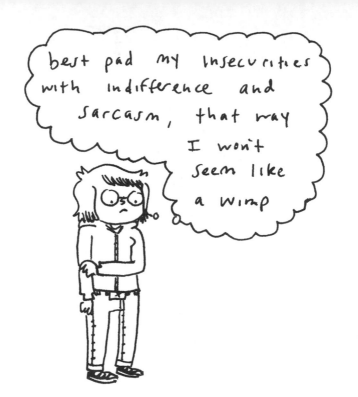

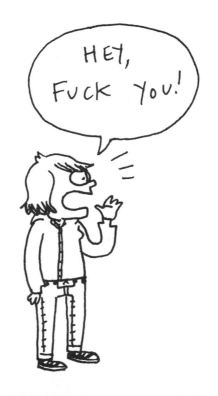

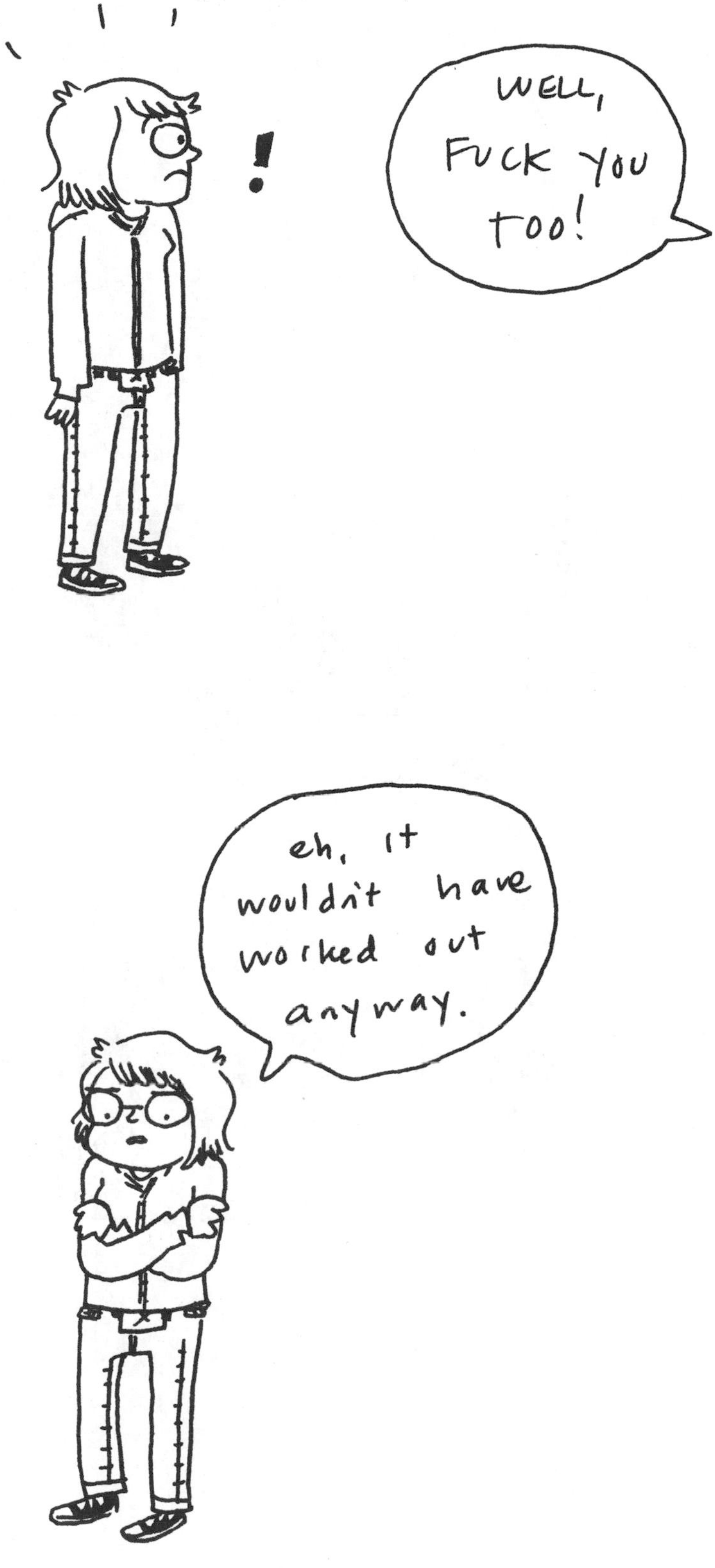
WELL, FUCK YOU TOO!
eh, it wouldn't have worked out anyway.

Blah Blah
psst, Liz, there's a dude at the bar you'll think is cute.
Yeah, that's an ex boyfriend who hates me.
oops. But I wasn't wrong...

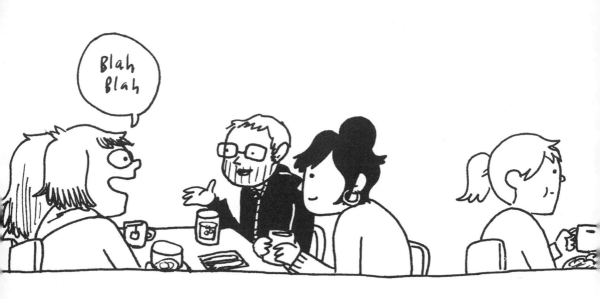

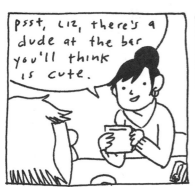

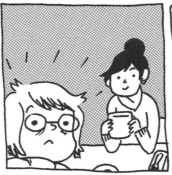

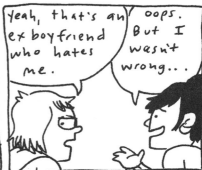

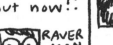

OCD CUPID

Checkin' you out now!:

 RAVER MON 34/M/S

 MUSCLES 2487 23/M/S

POETS LOVER 48/M/S

BEARDO 27:

Hey Liz, I'm excited to meet you tonight. You're still down to meet at Diesel at 7:30, right? You'll know it's me because I have a beard and glasses and I'll be wearing a flannel shirt. See yah soon!

oof. I hate the awkward meeting-some-one-for-the-first-time, not-sure-if-it's-them, looking-around-the-coffeeshop-thing.

well, here goes nothing...

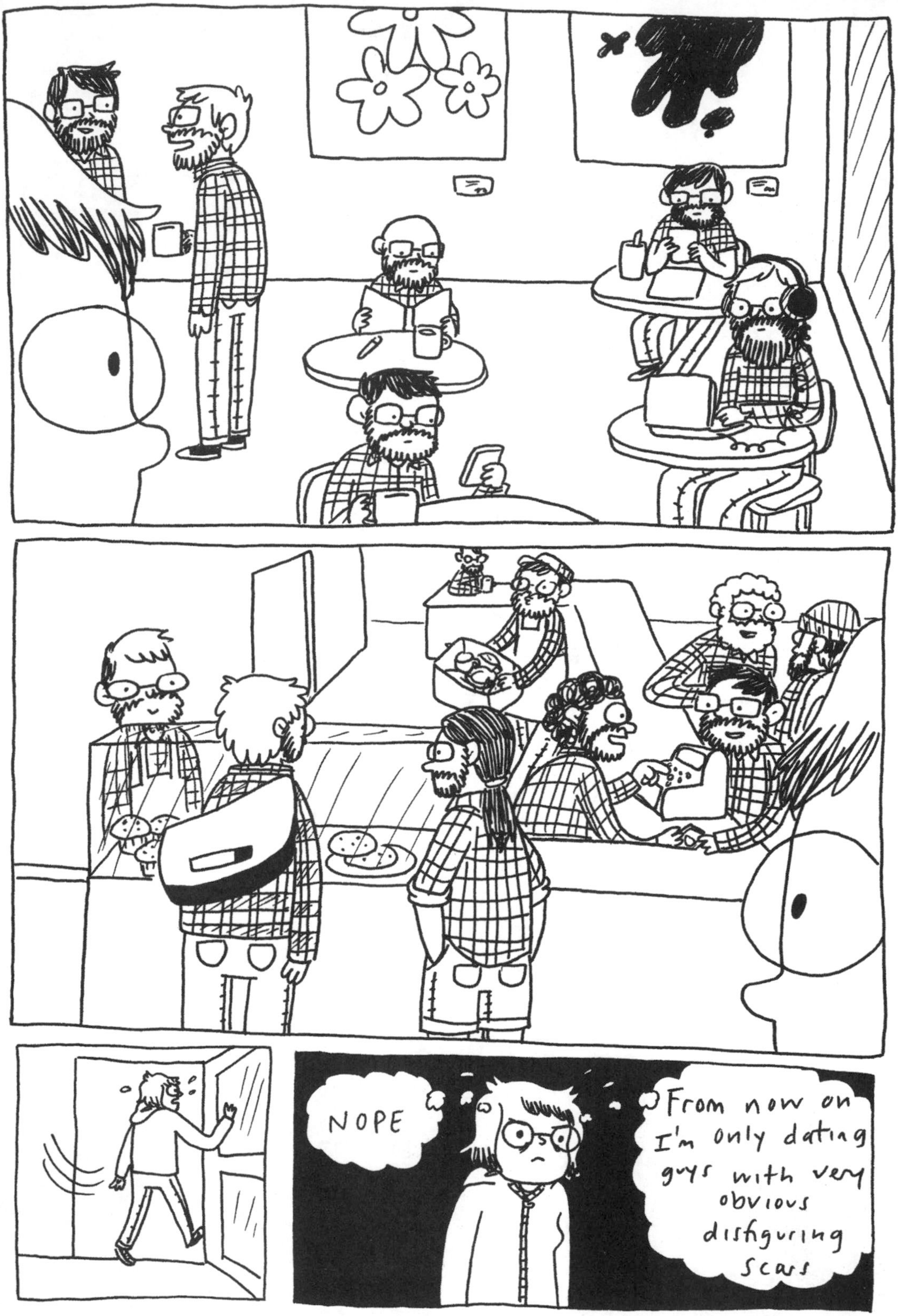
NOPE
From now on I'm only dating guys with very obvious disfiguring scars

A Brief History of my OK CUPID Dates

#1 LEIF

LEIF was a photographer whose main interest was shooting live hardcore shows. His username referenced a mid-90's hardcore band that was slightly obscure, so we hit it off over that. It took about 2 months of messaging to set up a date.

we had coffee and it was fun!

10,000 WAYS TO DIE!

BUFFY!

obscure Santa Fe band!

Mutual friends!

and he wanted to hang out again

snagged him

Hey Liz, That was cool, let's hang out again soon

But it took an additional 2 months to set up another date, again at a coffeeshop

he's pretty funny

blah blah blah

then we walked to the record store

METAL

But when it came time to say goodbye...

Thanks for hanging out again. I had fun.

Yeah! Hopefully 2 months doesn't go by before we hang out again.

Oh yeah? Well not everyone has the luxury of working from home and making their own schedule.

I am deeply offended. I told this guy I like him and WTF?

Hey buddy, just shoot for the stars and maybe someday your dreams will come true, too.

fucker

condesention pat ↓

and I never heard from him again. I've run into him a few times and he always claims to be:

VERY BUSY

as if I care, dude.

2   SETH

SETH contacted me because he found my profile to be "entertaining" and I thought his was acceptable enough, so we went on a date. He was so eager that our meet-up happened just 2 days after our first message exchange.

he seemed reluctant to pick an activity so we just sat on a bench

uh, so...

...

despite his extreme shyness, I did get this nugget of info:

I got my ex pregnant but she miscarried and then we broke up so I moved here.

overshare, much?

The date was going very poorly, but I felt bad ending it after only a half an hour on a park bench, so I suggested we get a drink, hoping that maybe he'd loosen up and be less debilitatingly nervous

but it didn't get any better

so, do you like any bands? music?

uh, um, well... I dunno. who do you like?

then he ordered jalapeno poppers and ate NONE of them

this is so awkward. I must leave now

he paid for my drink despite my protestations (because a fool and his money are soon parted) and he walked me home (about 2 miles) despite my protestations because apparently he just can't take a hint.

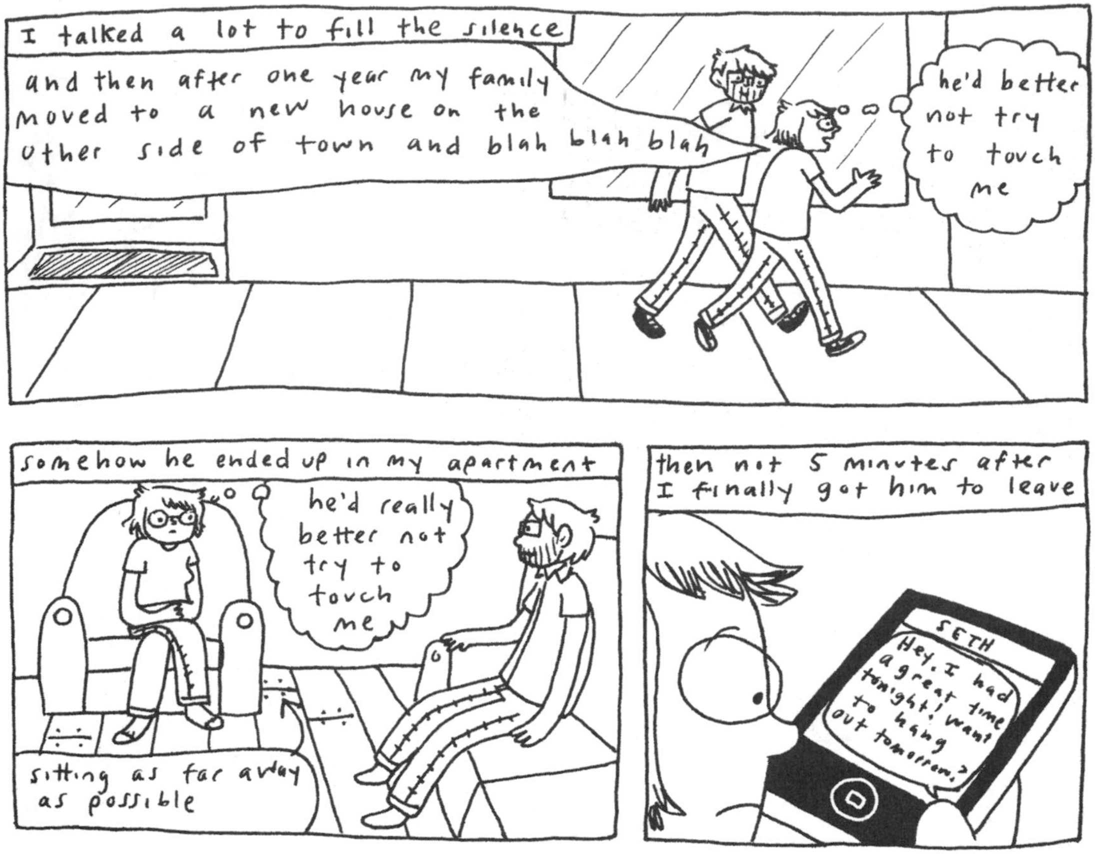
I talked a lot to fill the silence
and then after one year my family moved to a new house on the other side of town and blah blah blah
he'd better not try to touch me
somehow he ended up in my apartment
he'd really better not try to touch me
sitting as far away as possible
then not 5 minutes after I finally got him to leave
SETH
Hey, I had a great time tonight! Want to hang out tomorrow?

But my friends wouldn't believe that the problem with the date was my shy-guy suitor

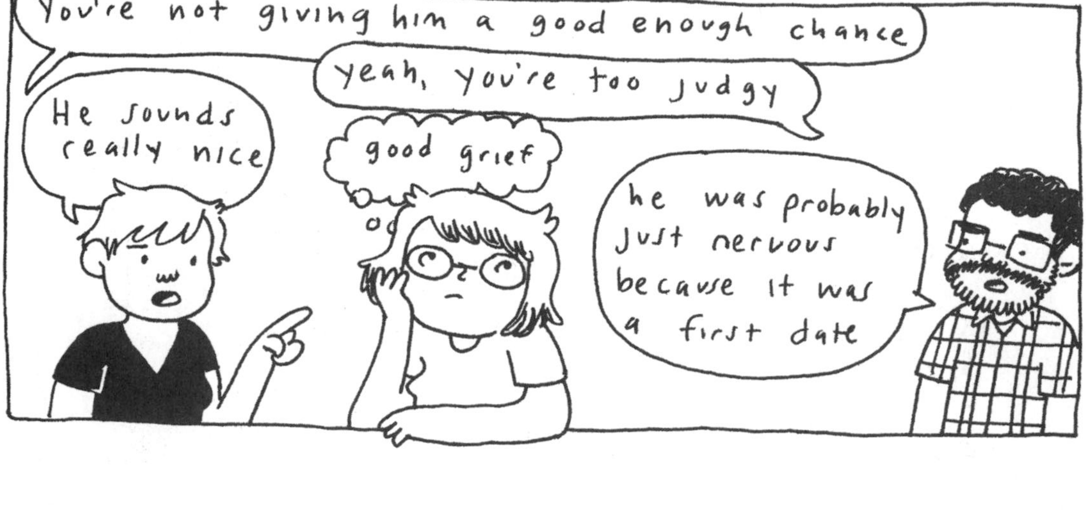
You're not giving him a good enough chance
yeah, you're too judgy
He sounds really nice
good grief
he was probably just nervous because it was a first date

and that is how, against my better judgement, I ended up on date #2 with SETH

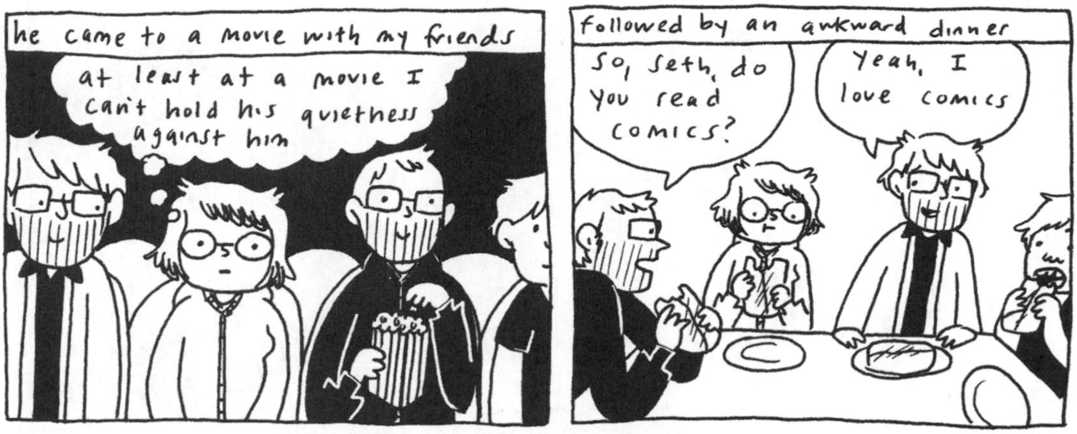
he came to a movie with my friends
at least at a movie I can't hold his quietness against him
followed by an awkward dinner
So, Seth, do you read comics?
Yeah, I love comics

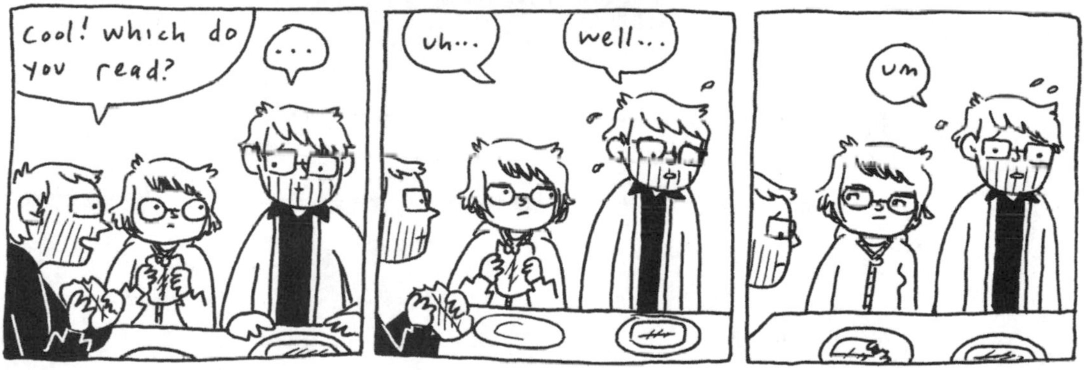
Cool! which do you read?
...
uh...
well...
um

and that was the end of my patience. Not being able to engage in even the simplest of conversations is a deal breaker. I sent him and his uneaten burrito home early

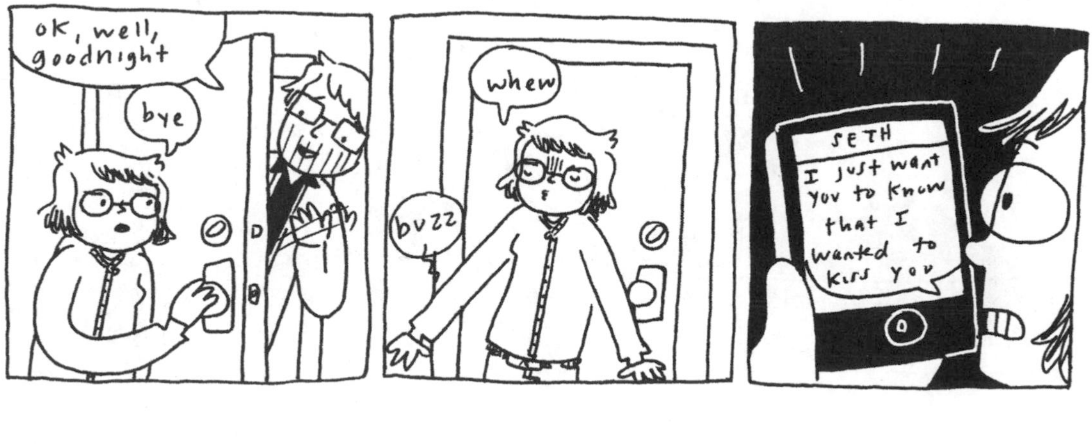
ok, well, goodnight
bye
whew
buzz
SETH
I just want you to know that I wanted to kiss you

send
SETH
I'm sorry. I don't have kissy feelings for you
Yeah, "my loss"
buzz
SETH
It's your loss, I've been told I'm a really good kisser.

#3 JOSH

JOSH was an acquaintance who I started messaging after I noticed he had looked at my profile. He was very cute and funny, and was already in the punk scene so we kind of had that in common. We messaged for about a month before getting coffee.

I had a good time, but I didn't expect to hear from him again
Imagine my surprise when he texted me the next day!
So, on the scale of going to the dentist or waiting in line at the post office, how bad was hanging out with me?

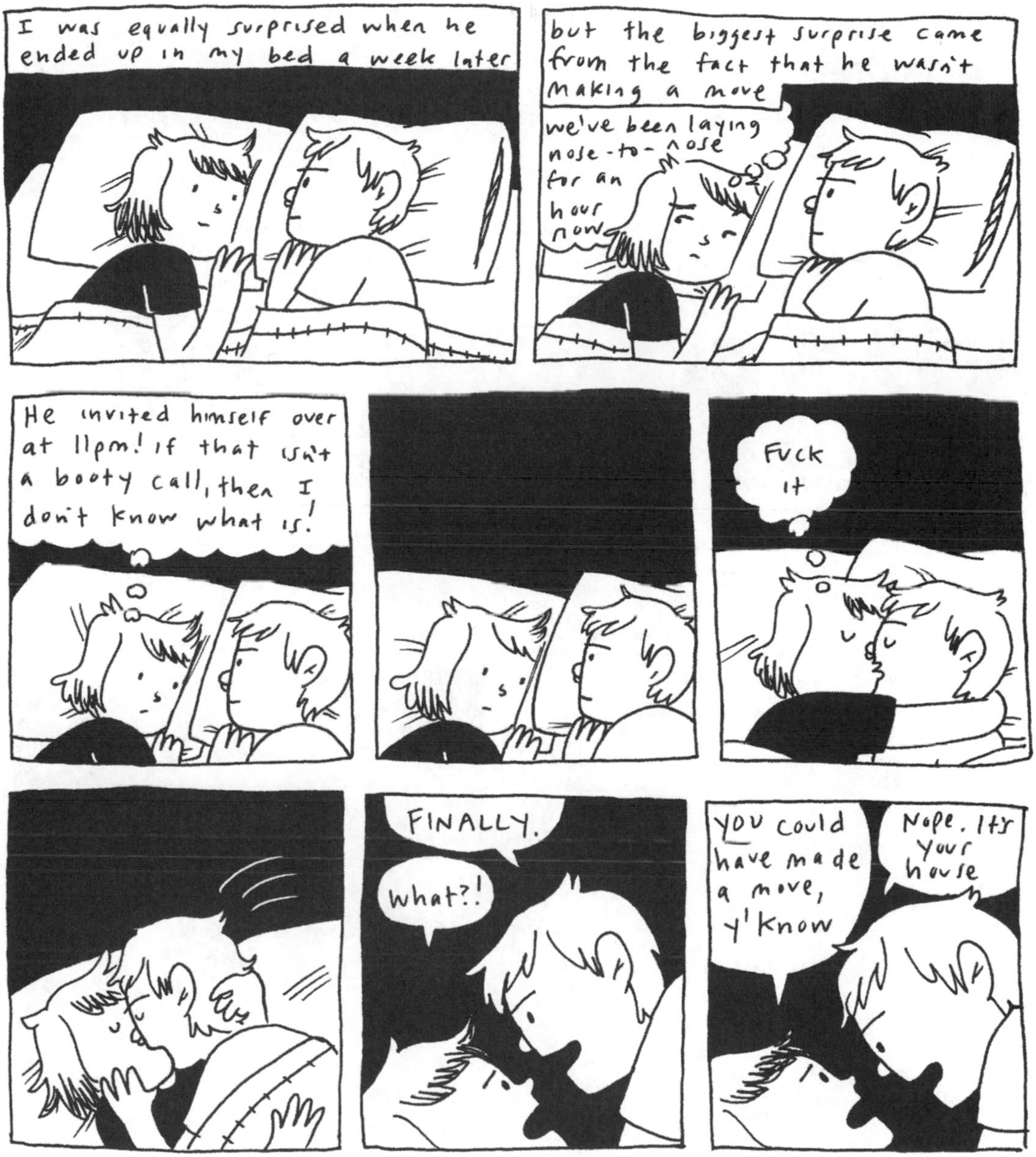
I was equally surprised when he ended up in my bed a week later
but the biggest surprise came from the fact that he wasn't making a move
we've been laying nose-to-nose for an hour now
He invited himself over at 11pm! if that isn't a booty call, then I don't know what is!
Fuck it
FINALLY.
what?!
YOU could have made a move, y'know
Nope. It's your house

That interaction right there set the stage for how the rest of my dates with JOSH would play out

he told me I could never come to his house.

Sorry, but it's too punk, you couldn't handle it.

he refused to ever pick a place to eat even though he had dietary restrictions

we can go out but you have to pick a place. I don't do that.

and we only hung out if I pursued him

I'm bored

well, you could ask me to hang out with you instead of baiting me into asking you to hang out with me

I wasn't really surprised when he initiated a conversation about "what we were" to tell me he didn't want to be my boyfriend

Are you seeing someone else?

NO

Do you want to be?

...NO

and I wasn't surprised at all a week later when he told me over email that he was actually seeing someone else

You could have been honest when I asked, dick.

One would assume that after these experiences had left a bad taste in my mouth I would no longer have an appetite for the human horror buffet that is OK Cupid, but just like Jello, there was room for more

#4 ROD

My thing with ROD was purely a rebound from my non-relationship with JOSH. ROD was someone I had met a few times through friends, and although I wasn't attracted to him, we had a lot in common on paper so I figured "why not?"

Things got off to a good start

Hello?

Hey, it's Rod! Do you want to meet at this diner before the record fair. It's really close...

Yeah, that sounds great

after SETH and JOSH's inability to make plans, it was a breath of fresh air to let ROD lead the way

This diner is pretty good!

Yeah, I love Diners! I research their history

logically, I should have been into ROD: he had interesting ideas for dates, he called more than he texted, and he genuinely wanted to have a good time, but I just didn't have a crush on him

I had a great time

Yeah, it was fun

...

eh heh, goodnight.

and he was a HORRIBLE kisser

ROD seemed gung-ho to hang out with me, and although I wasn't on the same page, I felt like I should give it a fighting chance (lest I once-again be deemed "too judgy"). But soon...

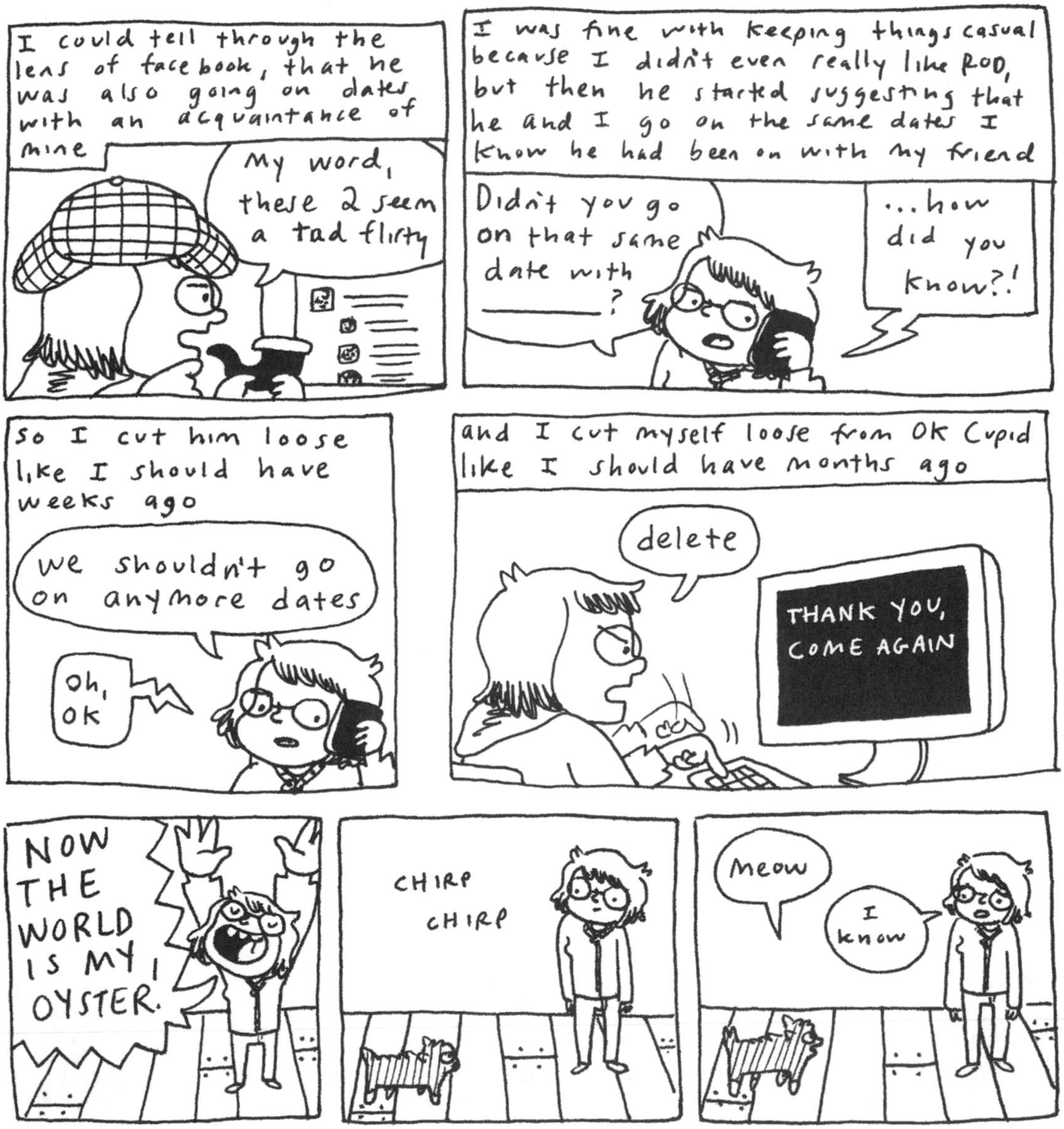

I could tell through the lens of facebook, that he was also going on dates with an acquaintance of mine
My word, these 2 seem a tad flirty
I was fine with keeping things casual because I didn't even really like ROD, but then he started suggesting that he and I go on the same dates I know he had been on with my friend
Didn't you go on that same date with ______?
...how did you know?!
so I cut him loose like I should have weeks ago
we shouldn't go on anymore dates
Oh, OK
and I cut myself loose from OK Cupid like I should have months ago
delete
THANK YOU, COME AGAIN
NOW THE WORLD IS MY OYSTER.
CHIRP
CHIRP
Meow
I know

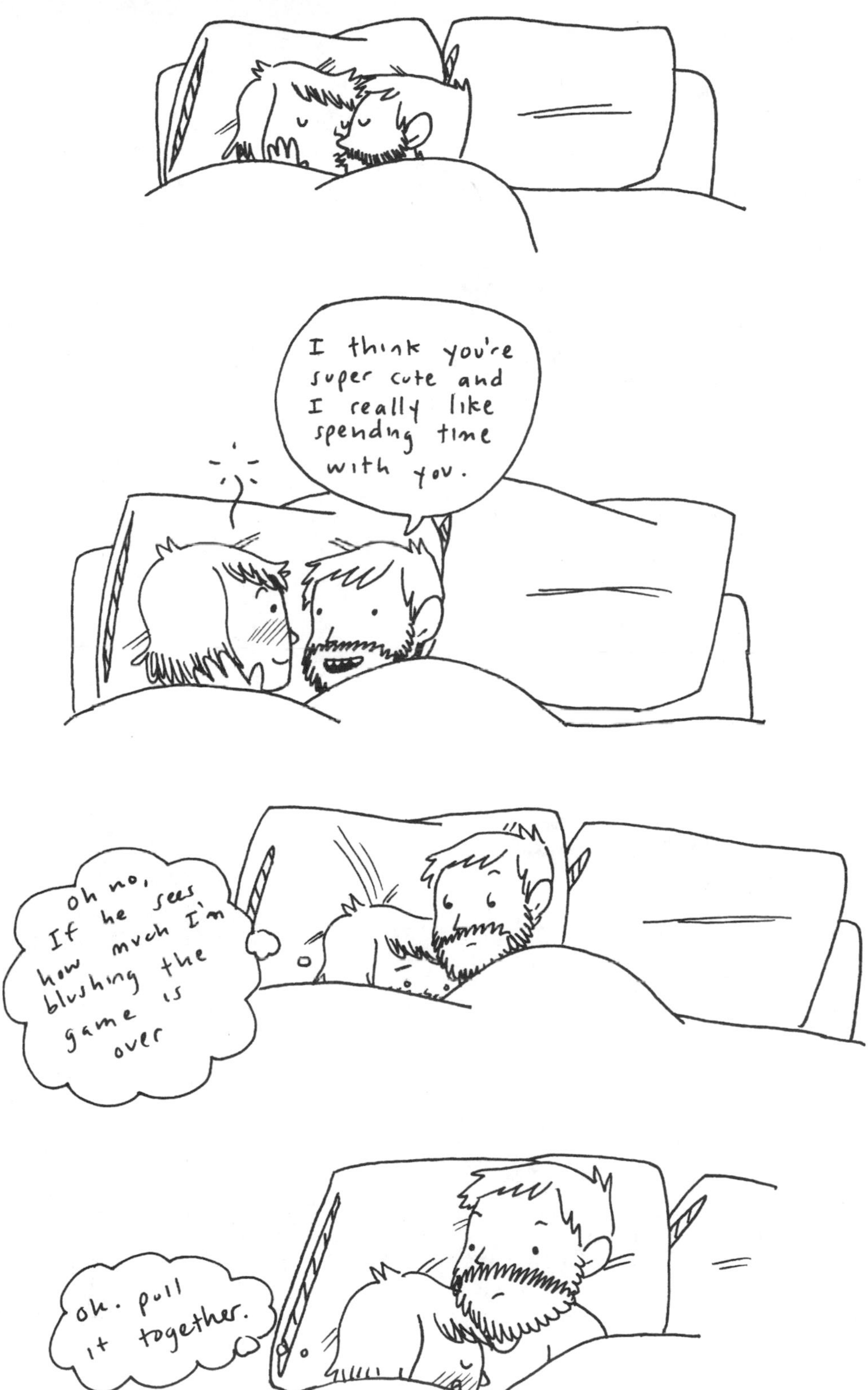
I think you're super cute and I really like spending time with you.
Oh no, If he sees how much I'm blushing the game is over
oh. pull it together.

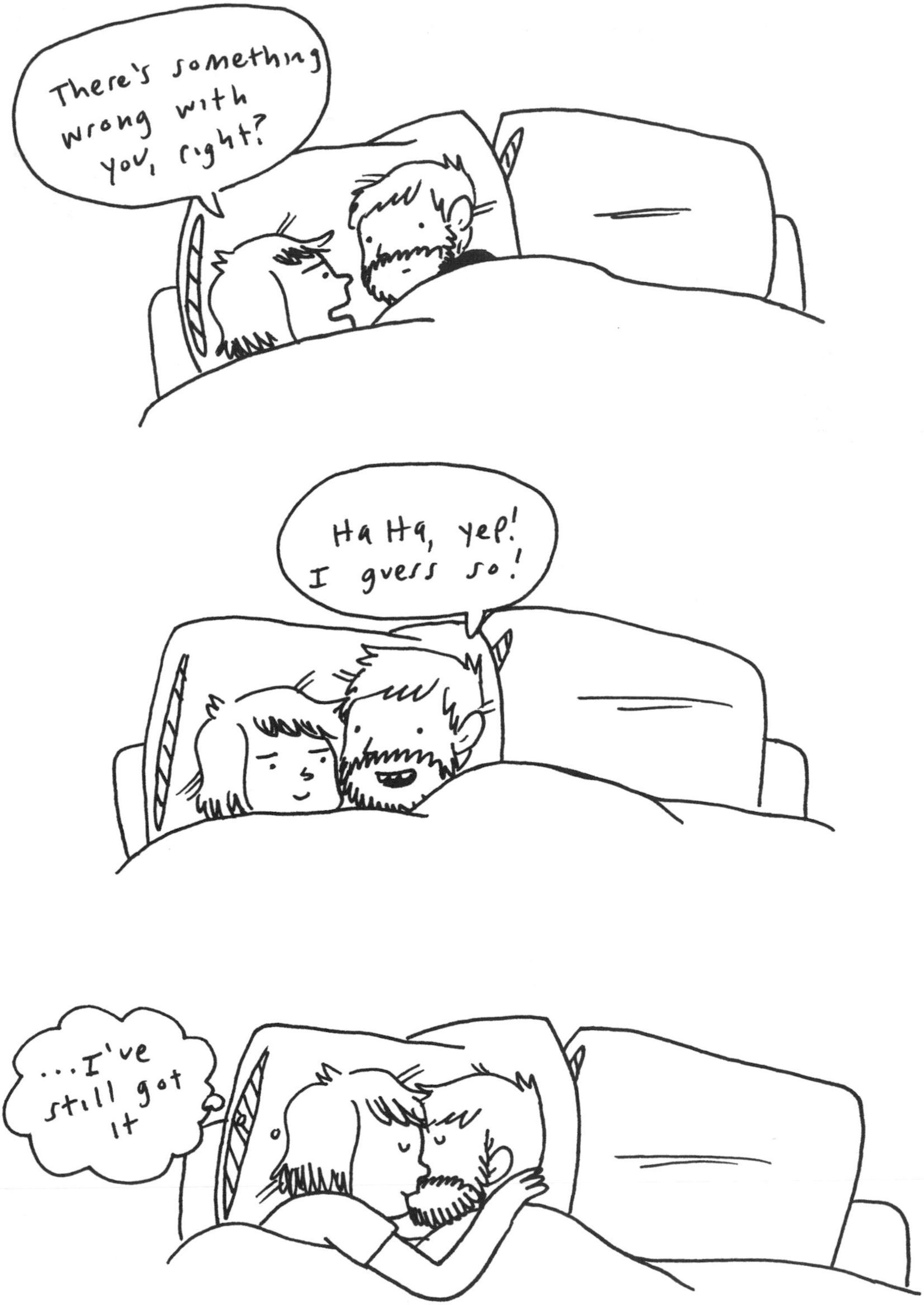
There's something wrong with you, right?
Ha Ha, yep! I guess so!
...I've still got it

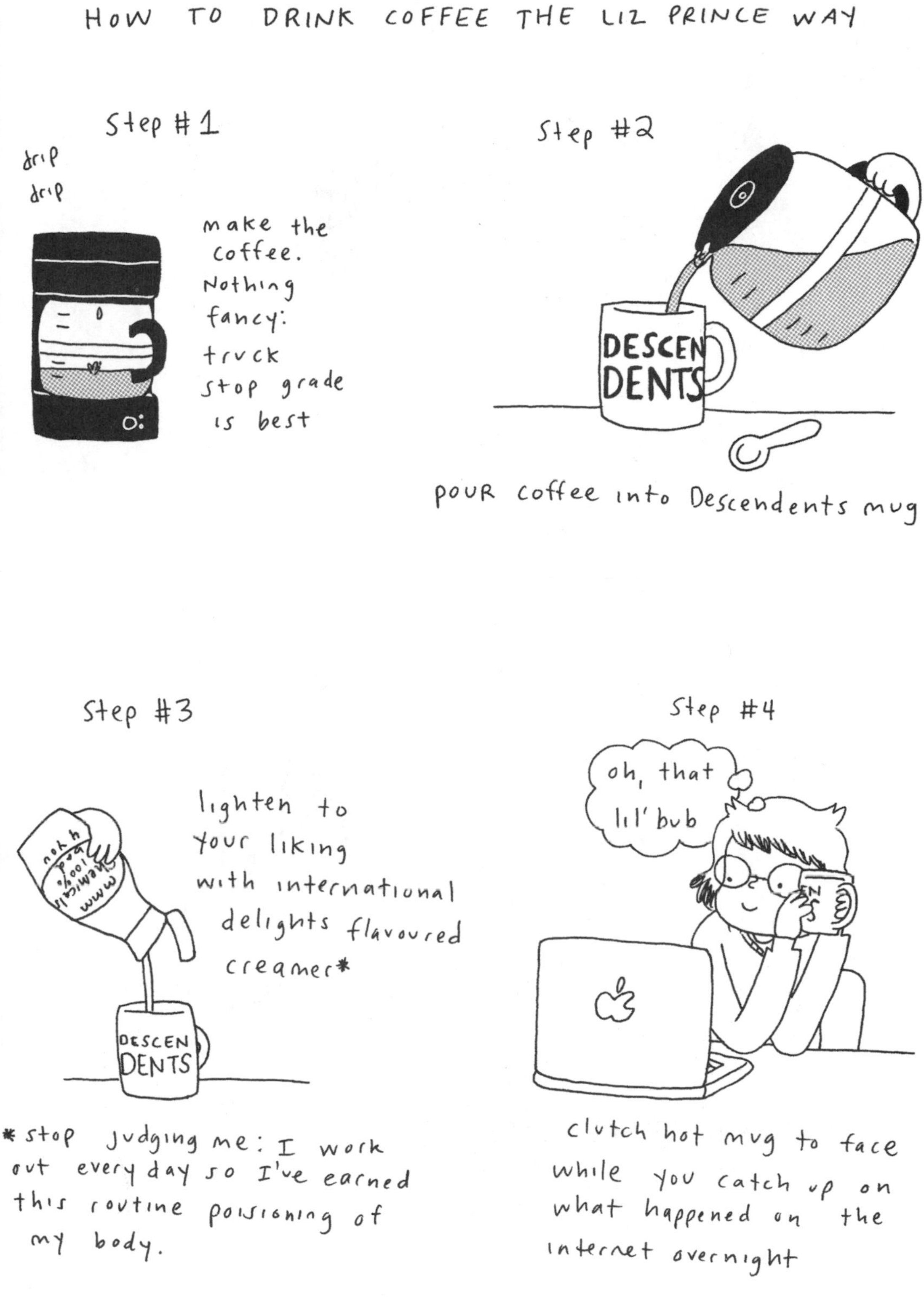
HOW TO DRINK COFFEE THE LIZ PRINCE WAY
Step #1
drip
drip
make the coffee. Nothing fancy: truck stop grade is best
Step #2
DESCEN DENTS
pour coffee into Descendents mug
Step #3
mmm chemicals 100% bad 4 you
lighten to your liking with international delights flavoured creamer*
DESCEN DENTS
* stop judging me: I work out every day so I've earned this routine poisoning of my body.
Step #4
oh, that lil' bub
clutch hot mug to face while you catch up on what happened on the internet overnight

Step #5 microwave coffee that went cold while reading facebook

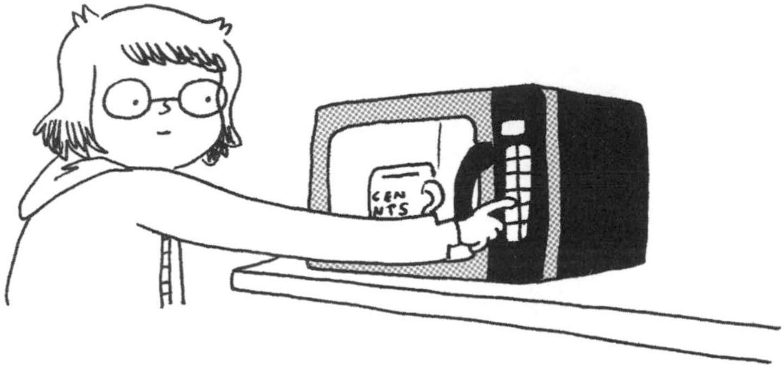

Step #6 Forget about coffee until the next time you go to use the microwave*

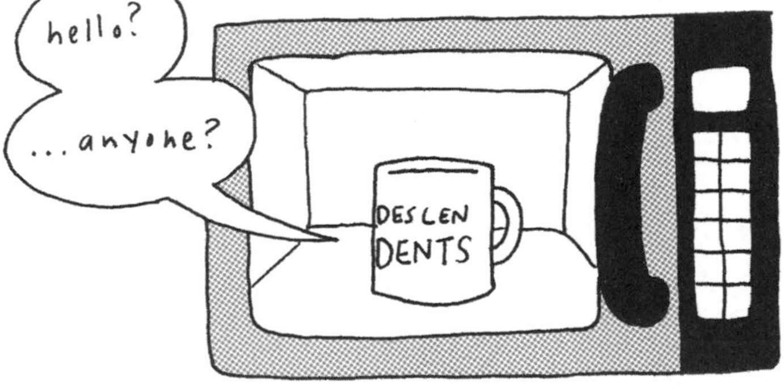
hello?
...anyone?
DESCEN
DENTS

* probably because you were reading facebook

Step #7 Die alone and leave a lasting legacy

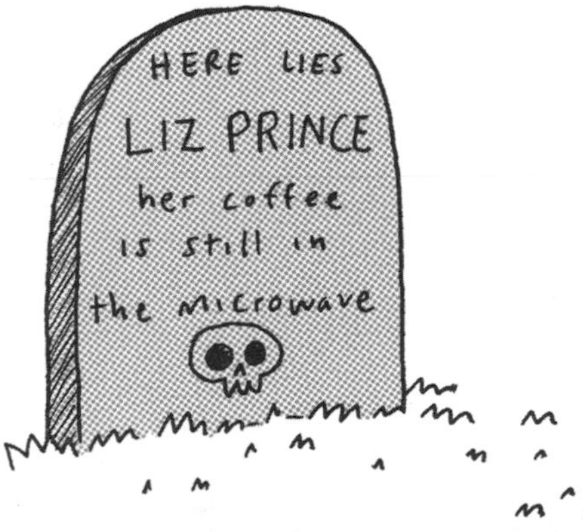
HERE LIES
LIZ PRINCE
her coffee
is still in
the microwave

AT LEAST UR NOT LIZ PRINCE
Aw c'mon! That's an awfully obscure reference

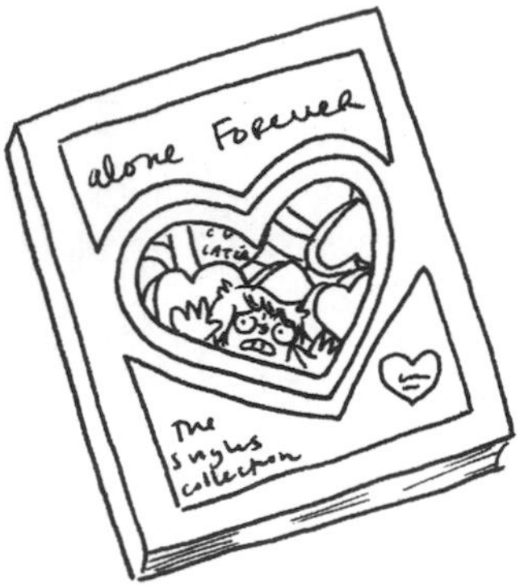
alone Forever
The singles collection

DON'T LET THIS BOOK BE **ALONE** ON YOUR SHELF, CHECK OUT THESE OTHER LIZ PRINCE TITLES FROM TOP SHELF PRODUCTIONS!

WILL YOU STILL LOVE ME IF I WET THE BED?

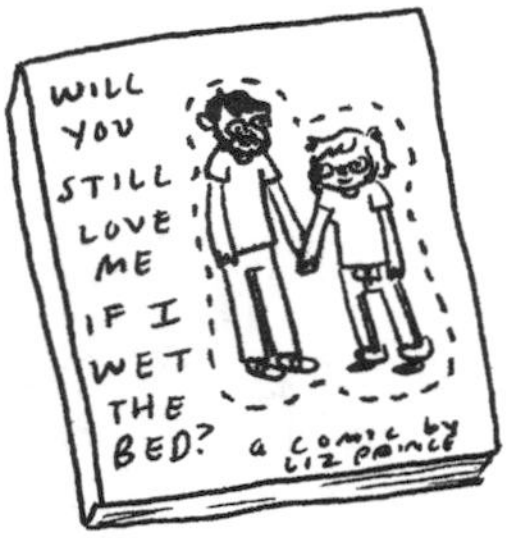
WILL YOU STILL LOVE ME IF I WET THE BED?
a comic by LIZ PRINCE

80 pages of cute, gross, and funny relationship comics

DELAYED REPLAYS

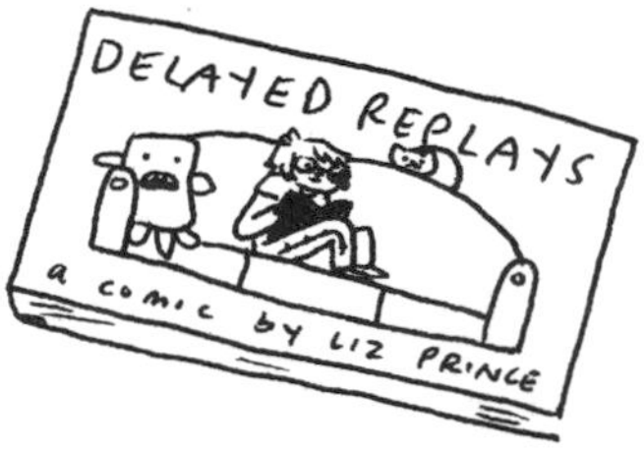
DELAYED REPLAYS
a comic by LIZ PRINCE

112 autobiographical gag strips

and an array of self published books and assorted merchandise available 24 hours a day on www.lizprincepower.com

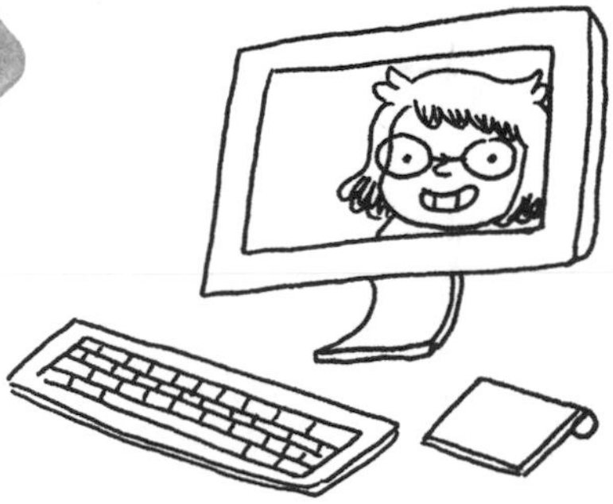